Congratulations! You're Still A Mess

Alex Telman

Published by Alex Telman, 2024.

CONGRATULATIONS! YOU'RE STILL A MESS

First edition. December 28, 2024.

ISBN: 979-8230376705

Written by Alex Telman.

Table of Contents

Author's Note

Dear Reader,

If you've ever felt stuck, frustrated, or like you're spinning your wheels, you're not alone. We've all been there. The struggle to break free from old habits, negative thinking, or a lack of motivation can feel endless. But what if I told you that everything you've been wanting—clarity, confidence, progress—can be achieved, not by waiting for the "perfect moment," but by taking deliberate, focused action?

This book isn't just another self-help guide filled with vague advice and feel-good affirmations. It's a blueprint for real change, designed to break you out of the cycle of procrastination and self-doubt and put you on a path to results—FAST. Inside, you'll find five powerful activities that will help you:

- **Make your thoughts positive** and stop letting negativity control your life.
- **Get results quickly** by implementing action steps that work and leave no room for excuses.
- **Grow your charisma** and start building deeper, more impactful relationships with others.
- **Fall in love with life again**, rediscovering joy and excitement in everyday moments.
- Plus two bonus activities—**Increased Energy Through Conscious Breathing** and a special tool for **Procrastinators**—that will help you tackle stress, boost your energy, and stay focused when you need it most.

This isn't a passive reading experience. It's a call to action. Each activity is practical, no-BS, and designed to challenge you. It's about taking full responsibility for where you are in your life right now and making the changes you need to move forward. No more waiting for the "right time" or for life to magically improve. The time for change is now.

What you'll get is a no-nonsense, actionable guide that will help you get out of your own way. I'll show you how to shift your mindset, take control of your emotions, and stop letting life dictate your choices. If you're tired of feeling stuck, if you're ready to stop making excuses and start living your best life—this book is for you.

If you're serious about change, but you're tired of fluff and superficial advice, this is the book that will actually help you make it happen. Are you ready to stop waiting for things to get better and finally create the life you truly want? Then take action, dive in, and let's get to work.

You're capable of more than you think. Let this book be your guide.

- Alex

Introduction

Let's set the record straight: this is not your typical self-help fluff. If you thought this book would be full of vague affirmations, "finding your inner peace," or making you feel good while sipping on organic smoothies, you've picked up the wrong book. I'm not here to sugarcoat things, coddle your ego, or promise you that everything will magically fall into place. What I'm here to do is help you break free from the mental mess that's been holding you back so you can actually start living the life you've been pretending to want.

This is not a collection of feel-good quotes to hang on your wall. If you're tired of feeling stuck, frustrated, and like you're running in circles, then you're in the right place.

What you're about to engage in is real work—difficult, but transformative work. This isn't a quick fix or a shortcut. What I'm offering you is a practical, no-nonsense guide that will help you stop getting in your own way and start making real, meaningful progress in your life.

We all have areas of our lives that feel like a mess. That's normal. The key difference is, you're done settling for the status quo. You've stopped pretending that everything's fine when deep down you're drowning under the weight of your own thoughts, habits, and decisions. And now, you're ready to take action and do something about it.

Here's the deal: life won't suddenly become perfect, and no one is promising that. But I will help you stop wasting time on things that don't matter and focus on what really does. You've been letting life happen to you for too long—letting other people dictate your mood, choices, and actions. It's time to flip the script. It's time to take control, and I'm here to show you how.

By picking up this book, you're making a commitment to face the truth. You're ready for some real feedback about what's been holding you back. If that doesn't sound like your cup of tea, that's okay—this book isn't for everyone. But if you're tired of being stuck and know something has to change, then keep reading.

So, how's your life going right now? How many times have you tried to "fix" things, only to end up feeling even more frustrated? How many times have you said, "I'll figure it out later," only for later to turn into "never"?

It's time to get out of that cycle. No more excuses. No more waiting for the "perfect moment." This is your wake-up call. It's time to start making changes that actually matter, and I'm here to show you how.

This book is built on four powerful activities that will get you out of your head and into action:

- **Activity 1: How to Make Your Thoughts Positive**
- **Activity 2: How to Get Results Fast**
- **Activity 3: How to Grow Your Charisma**
- **Activity 4: How to Fall in Love with Life Again**
- **Bonus Activity: Increased Energy Through Conscious Breathing**
- **Bonus Activity for Procrastinators**

Each activity is designed to help you shift your mindset, improve your habits, and start seeing real results. The goal is to take action—no fluff, no excuses. Whether you go through these activities in a few days or take your time, you'll walk away with practical tools that will help you break free from old patterns and start creating the life you actually want.

So, are you ready to stop wasting time? Good. Let's dive in. But here's the catch: I'm not going to tell you what you want to hear. I'm going to tell you what you *need* to hear. And sometimes, that might be uncomfortable. But trust me, it's the kind of discomfort that gets results.

Activity 1: Getting Rid of Negative Thinking

The Perfect Thought Activity

Want to change your life? Start with your thoughts. Every day, your mind is bombarded with a constant flood of chatter. Some of it's useful. Most of it's just noise. And you know exactly what I'm talking about—those random, unwanted thoughts that sneak in and tell you that you're not enough, that you're bound to fail, or that you'll never get it together. It's time to stop listening to that nonsense.

The **Perfect Thought Activity** is deceptively simple, but its power is undeniable. It's not about wishing those negative thoughts away or waiting for them to magically disappear. No, this time you're taking charge. You're not just listening to that inner critic—you're shutting it down before it has a chance to take root.

Let's break it down:

- "I'm not good enough."
- "I'm stupid."
- "I'm unattractive."
- "Nobody cares about me."
- "I'm a failure."

Those thoughts? They're lies. Lies you've been telling yourself for so long that you've started to believe them. But here's the truth: they're not facts. They're weaknesses in disguise. And this stops now.

Here's how you do it:

Listen to Your Thoughts.

First, slow down. I know, your brain is probably on a hamster wheel right now, but just for a moment, hit pause. Tune in. When those negative thoughts pop up—whether they feel brand new or like an old familiar tune—pay attention. It doesn't matter where they're coming from, whether they're tied to your past or just random, unhelpful brain junk. What matters is that you notice them.

You'll catch them easily:

- "I'm not good enough."
- "This is too hard. I'll never make it."
- "People are going to think I'm a failure."
- "Why do I always mess everything up?"

When you catch yourself thinking these, that's your cue. It's time to act.
Interrupt Those Thoughts.

The moment that negative thought pops into your head, don't sit there letting it marinate. Stop it cold. Right there. And here's your tool:

"This thought is perfect now."

Sounds simple, right? That's because it is. This isn't about fighting the thought or trying to argue with it. You're not trying to convince yourself the thought isn't true. That only gives it power. Instead, you're simply acknowledging it and refusing to let it control you.

Here's the secret: when you say, "This thought is perfect now," you're really saying, "I see you, but I'm not buying what you're selling. I'm fine. I'm still moving forward." It's like saying to your inner critic, "Nice try, but I'm not falling for it."

Examples:

- Thought: "My boss must hate me."
  Response: "Perfect. This thought is perfect now."
  No drama. No overthinking. You've dismissed it and moved on.
- Thought: "I'm so stupid."
  Response: "Yep, perfect. This thought is perfect now."
  Now you're in control. No self-loathing, no rehashing the past. Just a calm, confident dismissal.
- Thought: "I feel hopeless. I never do anything right."
  Response: "Perfect. This thought is perfect now."
  Neutralized. No agreement, no emotional reaction. Just a quiet "no,

thanks," and you're free to move on.

Why This Works:

It works because you stop feeding the beast. Every time you give in to these negative thoughts—whether you dwell on them, believe them, or let them dictate your mood—you're handing over your power. You let them settle in, and before long, they're no longer just passing thoughts. They become beliefs. But not anymore.

When you say, "This thought is perfect now," you're *neutralizing* it. You're not fighting it, but you're also not letting it pull you down. The fire fizzles out because you've stopped adding fuel. You simply refuse to engage with it.

The Bottom Line:

Want to change your life? Start with your thoughts. No more letting negative self-talk steer the ship. No more letting old wounds or outdated beliefs hold you back. You're going to interrupt. You're going to neutralize. You're going to move on.

Every time one of those destructive thoughts pops up, you're going to do this. Every. Single. Time.

It won't be perfect at first. That's okay. But as you keep practicing, you'll start to realize how much power you've been giving to those thoughts. And once that lightbulb goes on, you'll know you're done with them. You're done letting them run the show. And that's when the real change begins.

Building the Habit

Want this to work? Then you've got to build the habit. You can't just try this once and expect your life to magically change. This is about showing up every day. No excuses. No days off.

Start Slowly

You're not running a marathon today. You're just starting, so let's keep it simple. Begin by practicing the Perfect Thought Activity twice a day: once in the morning when you wake up, and once before you sleep. Why? Because these are the moments when your mind is most vulnerable. When you first wake up, your brain is still sluggish, and when you're winding down at night, it's easier for negative thoughts to creep in. But not anymore. Not on your watch.

Start by interrupting those negative thoughts as soon as you open your eyes in the morning, and then again before you close them at night. Just like a drill sergeant calling "attention," you're going to train your mind to snap out of its old, unhelpful habits. You're in charge now.

Daily Application

Once you've got the basics down, it's time to take this to the next level. Start applying it everywhere. In the middle of your workday, at the gym, with your family—whenever a negative thought pops up, you're going to stop it. No hesitation. No excuses. You hit pause and say, "This thought is perfect now."

The goal is to make this second nature. Don't just do it when it's convenient. Do it every single time. The more you practice, the less effort it will take, until eventually, it's as automatic as breathing.

Rewire Your Mind

This works. I promise. Over time, you'll literally rewire your brain. Those negative thoughts? They won't have the same power over you. You'll catch them before they even get a chance to settle in. But don't expect instant results. This takes time. It's a grind. Think of it like building muscle: one rep at a time.

Stay consistent. Be patient. This isn't a quick fix. The longer you stick with it, the more those negative thoughts will lose their grip on you. You'll realize something important: you weren't holding yourself back. Those thoughts were. But now? You're done with them.

The Result

So, what's the result? It's coming—but only if you do the work. If you stick with this every single day, you'll start to feel something shift. Big time.

Those thoughts that used to knock you off course? They won't have the same power anymore. They'll lose their grip on your emotions. Instead of spiraling into self-doubt or anxiety, you'll feel more grounded. More calm. More at peace.

That constant noise in your head? It'll quiet down. Why? Because you're taking away the fuel. You're not feeding those thoughts anymore. You're in control now. The more you practice, the more your mind will shift toward acceptance, peace, and clarity.

But listen up: don't expect this to happen overnight. This isn't a magic trick. No one reaches the top by taking shortcuts. It takes time, dedication, and grit. If you're looking for a quick fix, this isn't the book for you.

But here's the good news: if you keep showing up, if you keep doing the work, eventually your mind will stop being your enemy. It won't be a battleground of doubt and negativity anymore. It'll be calm, focused, and ready for whatever comes next.

Stick with it. That shift is coming.

Why the Perfect Thought Activity Works

This isn't just a feel-good exercise. This is about taking control of your mind. For far too long, you've let those negative thoughts call the shots. That ends now.

The Perfect Thought Activity is based on proven strategies: cognitive restructuring, mindfulness, and self-compassion. At its core, it's simple: interrupt those toxic thoughts and replace them with something empowering. You're rewiring your brain—and that doesn't happen overnight. If you think this is going to be easy, or that you can change without putting in the work, then this isn't for you.

But if you're ready to take control and put in the effort, you're going to see the results. It's time to stop letting those thoughts run your life. The real change is about to begin.

How It Works:

Cognitive Restructuring

This isn't just another "feel-good" method. Cognitive restructuring is a proven technique used in cognitive-behavioral therapy (CBT) to challenge and change negative thought patterns that mess with your head. These are the thoughts like:

- "I'm not good enough."
- "I'm a failure."
- "I can't do this."

Sound familiar? These thoughts sneak in and, before you know it, they take over. But here's the game-changer: Instead of letting them control you, you interrupt them. You don't argue, you don't try to fix them—you simply reframe them. You say:

"This thought is perfect now."

You're not agreeing with it. You're just not giving it any more power. You acknowledge it and move on. You take control. The thought may have popped up, but it's not hijacking your day.

Why This Works:

By saying, "This thought is perfect now," you neutralize it. You stop fighting and stop giving it emotional charge. Over time, you'll notice these negative thoughts won't have the same grip on you. You'll stop getting pulled into that endless cycle of self-doubt and fear. Instead, you'll replace them with more empowering thoughts, gradually rewiring your brain for change.

Example:

Imagine you get critical feedback at work. Instantly, your brain starts spiraling:

- "I'm not good enough."
- "I can't do anything right."
- "I'm going to get fired."

You catch these thoughts immediately. Instead of letting them take over, you interrupt them by saying:

"This thought is perfect now."

You've just broken the negative cycle. Next, you reframe:

- "I'm not good enough" becomes: *"That's just a thought. This thought is perfect now."*
- "I can't do anything right" becomes: *"I've learned from feedback before. This thought is perfect now."*
- "I'm going to get fired" becomes: *"This feedback is one moment. This thought is perfect now."*

Now, instead of spiraling, you create space for a more constructive mindset:

"I'm capable of learning and improving. This is an opportunity, not a threat. This thought is perfect now."

Result:

By consistently interrupting and reframing these negative thoughts, you break the old pattern. Instead of sinking into self-criticism, you create space for growth. Over time, this rewires your brain, making it easier to handle challenges without the emotional charge. You stop being controlled by negative thoughts—and that's how you change your mindset for good.

Mindfulness and Present-Moment Awareness

At the core of the Perfect Thought Activity is mindfulness. But don't worry, this isn't about sitting in silence for hours or living like a monk. Mindfulness is simply about being aware of your thoughts and emotions without judgment—being present in the moment, not letting your mind hijack it.

For too long, your mind has been in control, dragging you into emotional chaos. But mindfulness helps you step back, observe your thoughts, and realize they're just that—thoughts, not facts. They don't control you unless you let them.

Here's where the Perfect Thought Activity steps in: Instead of reacting emotionally to negative thoughts like "I'm not good enough" or "I'll never make it," you interrupt them with the phrase:

"This thought is perfect now."

This simple statement shifts your relationship with the thought. You're not fighting it or agreeing with it. You're just acknowledging it without letting it take over your emotions.

What Makes It Effective?

It weakens the grip of negative self-talk. By creating space between a thought and your emotional reaction, you take control. Over time, this becomes automatic. You'll stop letting negative thoughts dictate your emotions and start replacing them with more constructive ones.

Example:

Imagine you walk into a social event, and your mind starts spinning:

- "I'm not good at talking to people."
- "I'm going to look stupid."
- "What if they don't like me?"

Instead of getting lost in anxiety, you catch the thought:

"That's just a thought. It's not the truth."

You interrupt it with:

"This thought is perfect now."

You create space. Instead of spiraling, you stay grounded in the present moment, focusing on engaging with the people around you, not the hypothetical worries in your head.

Result:

You've broken the cycle. By interrupting and observing your thoughts without getting emotionally entangled, you reclaim your mental space and focus. With enough practice, this process becomes second nature, helping you stay calm and centered, no matter the situation. Mindfulness isn't about suppressing thoughts—it's about acknowledging them and not letting them control you.

Acceptance and Self-Compassion

Want to break free from negative thoughts? Stop fighting them. The more you struggle with thoughts like "I'm not good enough" or "I'm a failure," the more power you give them. Instead, practice **acceptance**.

The key is to acknowledge and accept your thoughts without engaging with them. When a negative thought arises, don't argue with it—just say, **"This thought is perfect now"**. This doesn't mean you agree with it, but you allow it to exist without letting it control you.

Self-compassion is also vital. Instead of criticizing yourself for having negative thoughts, treat yourself with kindness. Mistakes and flaws are part of being human. When you practice self-compassion, you stop fueling self-doubt and let go of perfectionism.

Example:

Imagine you've finished a big project, but instead of feeling proud, you start criticizing your work:

- "This isn't good enough."
- "I'm a failure."

Here's how to break the cycle:

- **Notice the Thought:** Acknowledge it without judgment.
- **Interrupt the Thought:** Use the phrase: "This thought is perfect now."
- **Practice Self-Compassion:** Be kind to yourself. Instead of saying, "I'm a failure," try, "This thought is perfect now. I did my best, and that's enough."
- **Embrace Acceptance:** Accept that imperfection is part of growth.

You're allowed to be human.

Result:

By accepting negative thoughts instead of fighting them, you stop the cycle of self-criticism. Over time, this practice helps you respond to setbacks with patience and compassion. Negative thoughts lose their grip, and you develop a mindset that's more resilient and empowering.

Self-compassion isn't weakness; it's strength. It's the strength to accept your imperfections and keep moving forward with confidence.

Interrupting Negative Thought Patterns (Summary)

Negative thoughts are automatic and can quickly become habitual, reinforcing self-doubt and anxiety. However, you don't have to let them control you. The **Perfect Thought Activity** helps interrupt these negative thought patterns before they spiral. Instead of arguing with or trying to suppress the negative thoughts, you simply acknowledge them, interrupt them, and reframe them.

Steps to Interrupt Negative Thoughts:

- **Notice the Thought**: Recognize when negative thoughts arise, such as "I'm a failure" or "I can't do this." Awareness is key.
- **Interrupt the Thought**: Immediately interrupt the negative thought with the phrase, **"This thought is perfect now."** This acknowledges the thought without giving it emotional weight, creating mental space.
- **Reframe the Thought**: Shift the narrative. For example, change "I'm a failure" to "That's just a thought. I am capable of growth. This thought is perfect now."
- **Release the Thought and Move On**: Once reframed, let go of the thought and refocus on the present moment. Don't dwell on it.

Why This Works:

Interrupting the negative thought cycle prevents the brain from reinforcing negativity, stopping the chain of self-doubt and anxiety. By reframing thoughts and shifting focus, you teach your brain that negative thoughts don't define you and that you can redirect your mind to more empowering perspectives.

Result:

With repeated practice, this method weakens the grip of negative thoughts. They'll still appear, but they won't carry the same emotional charge. Over time, your brain will naturally shift away from automatic negativity and toward more positive, empowering patterns. By interrupting negative thought loops, you take back control of your mind and stop being at the mercy of self-doubt.

Examples: Interrupting Negative Thought Patterns with the Perfect Thought Activity

Imagine you're gearing up for an important presentation at work. You've done the prep, you've rehearsed, but as soon as you step in front of the group, your mind starts spinning with negative thoughts:

- **"I'm going to mess this up."**
- **"I'm not prepared enough."**
- **"Everyone's going to think I'm a fraud."**

These thoughts are automatic. They arise quickly, almost like a knee-jerk reaction. They're familiar, old patterns of self-doubt that you've experienced in the past during high-pressure situations.

Here's how the *Perfect Thought Activity* works in this case:

- **Notice the Thought**: You catch yourself in the middle of this spiraling thought cycle. You notice the familiar wave of fear and self-doubt creeping in.
  "I'm going to mess this up."
  "I'm not prepared enough."

Right there, you **pause**. Instead of letting the negative thoughts take hold and derail you, you become **aware** of them as they arise.

- **Interrupt the Negative Thought**: Instead of letting these thoughts spiral into more anxiety, you **interrupt** the pattern. You don't ignore or fight the thought—you simply respond with:
  "This thought is perfect now."

This is a critical moment. By interrupting the negative cycle, you **disrupt** the automatic reaction. You don't let your mind take over and reinforce the pattern of **self-criticism** or **fear**. You simply acknowledge the thought, but you don't let it control you.

- **Shift the Focus and Reframe**: Now that you've interrupted the thought, you **reframe** it. You don't let it sit there and fester.

Preface your response to all the following thoughts with: "This thought is perfect now."

- Instead of **"I'm going to mess this up,"** you shift to: **"I've prepared, I know my material, and I can handle this."**
- Instead of **"I'm not prepared enough,"** you remind yourself: **"I've done the work. I'm ready. I trust myself."**
- Instead of **"Everyone's going to think I'm a fraud,"** you tell yourself: **"I'm giving my best. I don't need to be perfect, I just need to show up."**

- **Reset the Pattern**: By repeating this process of **interruption** and **reframing**, you've reset the negative thought pattern. You're no longer feeding it with more self-doubt or fear. Instead, you've broken the cycle and replaced it with a more **empowering** and **grounded** response.

Result: In this situation, you've successfully interrupted a deep-rooted negative thought pattern. These thoughts—"I'm going to mess this up," "I'm not good enough," "I'm a fraud"—are not new. They've likely been with you for years in high-pressure situations. But with the *Perfect Thought Activity*, you've broken the automatic cycle and replaced it with a more confident and focused mindset. Over time, this practice weakens the grip of those negative patterns. Each time you interrupt them, you build new neural pathways, which helps you respond to future challenges with **less fear** and **more confidence**.

This is **Interrupting Negative Thought Patterns** in action—when your mind starts to take you down the same old road of doubt, you **step in** and break the pattern before it can take over. Instead of reinforcing old habits of negative self-talk, you replace them with more constructive, confident thoughts. And over time, this rewires your brain to react **differently**—with calmness, resilience, and confidence in your abilities.

Rewiring the Brain with the Perfect Thought Activity

The **Perfect Thought Activity** utilizes the concept of neuroplasticity, which is the brain's ability to rewire itself through repeated practice. This process helps break negative thought patterns and replace them with more empowering, positive thoughts. Here's how it works:

Notice the Thought:

- **Catch the thought** as it arises. This step is crucial because negative thoughts often run on autopilot, unnoticed, reinforcing habitual anxiety. Being aware of these thoughts is the first step toward taking control over them.
- **Example**: Before giving a speech, you might automatically think, "I'm going to forget what I'm saying," or "What if I mess up?" These thoughts are conditioned, and noticing them helps break the automatic cycle.

Interrupt the Negative Thought:

- **Acknowledge the thought** with neutrality rather than reacting to it with fear or self-doubt. Use the phrase **"This thought is perfect now"** to interrupt the negative pattern.
- This helps prevent the thought from escalating into anxiety. By pausing and acknowledging the thought without agreeing with it, you create mental space, allowing your brain to stop reinforcing the old, negative neural pathway.

Reframe the Thought:

- **Shift the narrative** by reframing the negative thought into something more positive or realistic. This step is vital for creating new neural pathways.

- **Examples**:
  - Instead of "I'm going to forget what I'm saying," reframe it as: "I've prepared, and I can handle this."
  - Instead of "I'll look foolish," reframe it as: "Mistakes happen, and I can recover."
  - Instead of "What if they judge me?" reframe it as: "I'm here to share my message, and that's what matters."
- These reframes build new pathways that promote confidence and calmness.

Practice and Repetition:

- **Repetition is key** to rewiring the brain. Just as exercising a muscle strengthens it, repeatedly interrupting negative thoughts and reframing them helps to create healthier, stronger neural pathways.
- Over time, these new pathways become automatic, so situations that once triggered anxiety will start to trigger calmness and confidence instead.

Result:

Through regular practice, the brain shifts from reinforcing fear-based patterns to fostering more empowering, calm, and confident responses. This is how you use neuroplasticity to rewire your brain and break free from automatic negative thought cycles.

The Impact of Rewiring Your Brain

By practicing the Perfect Thought Activity consistently, you are actively rewiring your brain to respond differently to stress, anxiety, and negative thoughts. The key is to be patient- it takes time and repetition. But over time, you will begin to notice a **shift** in how your brain responds to challenges. The old, negative pathways will weaken, and new, healthier pathways will grow stronger.

Detachment from the Thought

The practice of **detachment** helps you break free from the cycle of negative thinking and regain control over your emotional and mental state. Here's how it works:

Understanding Detachment

- **Detachment** means recognizing that you are not your thoughts. Thoughts are temporary mental events, not reflections of your true self. Over-identifying with negative thoughts (e.g., "I'm a failure," "I'll never succeed") leads to pain and emotional chaos.
- **Mindful detachment** involves observing your thoughts without letting them define you or control your emotional state. The goal is to see thoughts as passing phenomena, not as truths about who you are.

Why Detachment is Empowering

- **Detachment** shifts your relationship with thoughts. Instead of getting caught in negative cycles, you become the observer of your thoughts, not their subject.
- Think of your mind as the **sky** and your thoughts as **clouds**—some dark, some light. The sky (you) remains unaffected by the clouds (thoughts), which come and go.
- By practicing detachment, you gain **mental clarity** and freedom from emotional turmoil. Thoughts no longer dictate your reactions or identity.

The Cycle of Over-Identification with Thoughts

- When you over-identify with negative thoughts, you internalize them and they become core beliefs. This leads to a **self-reinforcing cycle**: Negative thought → emotional reaction → self-criticism → reinforcement of the negative thought.
- This cycle traps you in past experiences and mistakes, preventing you from moving forward and cultivating new beliefs about yourself.

How Detachment Works in the Perfect Thought Activity

- **Notice the Thought**: Become aware of when negative thoughts arise (e.g., "I'm not good enough"). Don't react with guilt or self-criticism—just observe the thought.
- **Interrupt the Thought**: Use the phrase **"This thought is perfect now"** to break the cycle. This helps stop automatic over-identification and creates space between you and the thought.
- **Create Space**: By saying "This thought is perfect now," you pause and recognize that the thought is just that—a thought, not a truth. This creates **mental space**.
- **Detach and Move On**: Detach from the thought by letting it go. Don't dwell on it or believe it defines you. Allow the thought to pass, like a cloud, and move forward without emotional attachment.

The Power of Being the Observer

- The key to detachment is becoming the **observer** of your thoughts rather than being identified with them. This allows you to maintain **emotional balance** and **mental clarity**.
- By observing, you gain the power to **respond consciously** to situations, instead of reacting automatically to negative thought patterns.

Embrace Detachment for Freedom

- Practicing detachment frees you from the power of negative thoughts. You acknowledge them without allowing them to control your emotions or behavior.
- Over time, this practice helps you understand that thoughts are **fleeting** and do not define your identity. **You are not your thoughts**—you are the observer, and through this awareness, you create peace and emotional stability.

The practice of detachment through the Perfect Thought Activity empowers you to break free from negative thought cycles. By observing your thoughts, interrupting negative patterns, and reframing them, you regain control of your mind and emotions. This process leads to a deeper sense of **self-awareness**, **clarity**, and emotional **freedom**.

Examples: Detachment from the Thought using the Perfect Thought Activity

Imagine you're at work and receive **critical feedback** from your manager about a recent project. The feedback isn't harsh, but it stings because you've invested a lot of effort into the project. Immediately, negative thoughts arise, such as:

- "I'm terrible at this job."
- "I always mess up; no one respects me."
- "This proves I'm not good enough."

These thoughts can feel heavy and personal, and they trigger negative emotions like **embarrassment**, **frustration**, or **defensiveness**. However, rather than allowing these thoughts to define you or spiral into self-judgment, you can use the **Perfect Thought Activity** to detach from them. Here's how it works:

Steps for Detachment:

Notice the Thought:

The first step is to **catch** the negative thought as soon as it arises.

- Example: *"I'm terrible at this job."*
- Recognize that this is an **automatic thought**—one you've likely experienced before. It's a **habitual pattern** that doesn't define you. Instead of identifying with it, you **pause** and notice it for what it is: just a thought.

Interrupt the Negative Thought:

Instead of reacting emotionally to the thought, you interrupt it by saying:

- **"This thought is perfect now."**
- This doesn't mean you agree with the negativity, but rather that you **acknowledge** the thought without allowing it to control you. You are creating space between the thought and your emotional reaction,

effectively **disengaging** from it. This step is about saying: *"This is just a thought. It doesn't define me."*

Create Detachment from the Thought:
After interrupting the thought, you detach from it by recognizing that:

- The thought is **temporary** and **doesn't define your worth.**
- Example reframing: "That's just a thought. It's not the truth. I can learn from this feedback and improve."
- Instead of internalizing it as a reflection of your identity (e.g., "I always mess up"), you simply observe it without judgment. You choose not to **merge** with the thought, recognizing it as a fleeting mental event that doesn't dictate who you are.

Recenter Yourself:
With detachment in place, you can **refocus** on the present moment and move forward with clarity:

- Example reframing: "I'm not terrible at my job. I'm here to grow, and this feedback is part of that process."
- Another reframing: "I'm not a failure. I'm someone who learns from mistakes and gets better with practice and feedback."

Result:

By practicing **detachment**, you've taken the **emotional power** away from the negative thought. Instead of letting it overwhelm you with self-doubt or shame, you've **observed** the thought, acknowledged it, and chosen not to let it define you. This creates **mental space** between the thought and your emotional reaction, allowing you to process feedback without being trapped in a spiral of negativity.

Over time, with regular practice, you'll find that detaching from negative thoughts becomes easier. You'll be better able to:

- **Observe** negative self-talk without reacting emotionally.
- Choose how to **respond** from a place of awareness, rather than being

swept away by self-criticism.

By using the **Perfect Thought Activity**, you'll strengthen your ability to **detach from judgments**, maintain **emotional clarity**, and avoid over-identifying with negative thoughts. This helps you stay centered and empowered, rather than being at the mercy of automatic, self-critical thinking.

Remember:

- **Detachment** means recognizing that thoughts are temporary and don't define you.
- **The Perfect Thought Activity** helps you break free from automatic negative patterns by creating **space** between thoughts and emotional reactions.
- By regularly practicing detachment, you regain control over your emotional state, allowing you to respond to feedback (or any situation) from a place of **empowerment**, rather than being consumed by negativity.

In essence, detaching from thoughts allows you to maintain emotional balance, making it easier to **learn, grow**, and **move forward** without being weighed down by self-judgment or fear.

You Are the Driver

In the end, the **Perfect Thought Activity** helps you take control of your mental and emotional life. You'll stop being a passive observer of your thoughts, letting them dictate your feelings and actions. Instead, you'll step into the driver's seat and actively choose how to respond to your thoughts.

You have the power to decide: **Will I let this negative thought control me, or will I control it?** Every time you practice this, you reinforce your ability to stay grounded and calm, no matter what negative thoughts arise. Over time, you'll stop being a slave to your mental patterns, and you'll start driving the bus.

This is the true **empowerment** that comes with consistent practice of the Perfect Thought Activity. You'll become more **resilient**, more **empowered**, and more **in control** of your life. Negative thoughts will no longer run the show—you will. And that is the ultimate freedom.

Preface your response to all the thoughts with: "This thought is perfect now."

Activity 2: Get Results Fast

The What? Activity: Clarifying and Acting on Your Thoughts

You've been stuck in a loop, endlessly circling around the same negative questions. Questions like:

- **"Why am I so stupid?"**
- **"Why do I always fail?"**
- **"Why can't I get anything right?"**

If these sound familiar, it's because **Why? questions** are often **dead ends**. They don't provide answers that help you move forward. Instead, they trap you in a cycle of rumination, self-blame, and frustration.

Here's the hard truth: asking **"Why?"** isn't going to make you feel better. It won't solve the problem, and it certainly won't lead you to a solution. Instead, it locks you deeper into the negative thinking process, making you feel worse rather than better.

For example:

- Asking **"Why am I stupid?"** doesn't give you insight or a roadmap for growth. It just reinforces a negative self-image and leaves you feeling powerless and stuck.
- Asking **"Why do I always fail?"** doesn't show you how to change or improve. It just adds layers to your frustration and self-doubt.

You're not going to find clarity or progress by endlessly repeating Why? questions. What you need is a shift in perspective.

The Power of What? Questions

The solution is simple: **Stop asking "Why?" and start asking "What?"**

What? questions open the door to **action, clarity,** and **empowerment.** They help you focus on what you can do, what you can change, and what steps you can take. Instead of getting trapped in endless self-criticism, you move into problem-solving mode.

What? questions shift your mindset from being passive and stuck to active and empowered. They help you direct your energy toward practical solutions, instead of staying stuck in a mental whirlpool of blame and helplessness.

How the What? Activity Works

The **What? Activity** is designed to help you break free from the cycle of rumination and self-doubt, replacing **Why?** questions that trap you in frustration with **What?** questions that lead to actionable solutions. Here's a breakdown of how to use this activity effectively:

Recognize the Why Question

The first step is awareness. You need to notice when you're asking a **Why? question** that gets you nowhere. These kinds of questions don't offer clarity or solutions. Instead, they trap you in cycles of self-blame, frustration, or confusion. Some common examples include:

- "Why am I always messing up?"
- "Why am I so lazy?"
- "Why do I keep failing?"

These questions keep you stuck. They don't propel you forward. They only amplify self-doubt and make you feel worse. So, the key here is to **catch yourself** when you're spiraling into these **Why?** questions and recognize what's happening. This is your signal to shift gears.

Interrupt with a What Question

The next step is to interrupt the cycle of negativity. When you catch yourself asking a **Why? question, immediately replace it with a What? question.**

Here are some examples of how to reframe your thoughts with **What?** questions:

- Instead of **"Why am I stupid?"**, ask **"What do I need to learn to improve?"**
- Instead of **"Why do I always fail?"**, ask **"What can I do differently next time?"**
- Instead of **"Why am I so lazy?"**, ask **"What action can I take right now to make progress?"**

The power of the **What? question** is that it opens up possibilities. It directs your focus toward **solutions**, not problems. It's no longer about looking for an explanation for why you're stuck. It's about looking for a way out of the cycle.

Clarify the What Question

Once you've switched to a **What? question**, the next step is to **clarify** it. The more specific and detailed your question, the clearer and more actionable your answer will be. Vague questions like **"What should I do?"** or **"What do I need to change?"** will leave you stuck, unsure of what to do next. So, get specific.

Here are some ways to make your **What? questions** more actionable:

- If you ask **"What do I need to learn?"**, you might clarify it with: **"I need to learn how to manage my time better."**
- If you ask **"What can I do differently next time?"**, you might clarify it with: **"I need to focus on one task at a time instead of multitasking."**
- If you ask **"What action can I take right now?"**, you might clarify it with: **"I'm going to write down a list of priorities and tackle the most important one first."**

The more specific you can get, the clearer your path forward becomes. **Specificity turns vague worries into actionable steps.**

Act on the Answer

This is the key step: once you have a clear, specific answer to your **What? question, you need to act on it**. The **What? Activity** isn't about endless thinking or overanalyzing—it's about moving from thought to action.

Here are some examples of how to take action:

- If you realize you need to **learn how to manage your time better**, take immediate steps like signing up for a time-management course, downloading a time-tracking app, or reading a book on the topic.
- If you identify that you need to **focus better**, start practicing techniques like **deep work** or using a **Pomodoro timer** to help you concentrate on one task at a time.
- If you discover that you just need to **make progress**, don't wait for motivation. Take the first step right now, no matter how small. Whether it's jotting down a list of tasks or setting a timer for 15 minutes to start working, just begin. Action leads to momentum.

The point is: stop dwelling on the **Why?** questions and move into the **What?**—then **act**. The more you act, the more you'll start to see **real change**. The momentum will build as you take consistent steps toward improvement, and soon the cycle of rumination will become a thing of the past.

Example Scenario

Let's put this into practice with a real-life scenario. Suppose you've been feeling stuck at work. You find yourself asking:

- **"Why am I so disorganized?"**
- **"Why do I keep missing deadlines?"**
- **"Why can't I get anything done?"**

These **Why?** questions aren't helpful—they only increase frustration. Instead, shift to **What?** questions.

- **"What can I do to become more organized?"**
- **"What changes can I make to meet deadlines?"**
- **"What's one small thing I can do right now to start working more effectively?"**

After clarifying these questions, you might come up with specific answers like:

- **"I can start using a planner to organize my tasks each morning."**

- **"I can break down projects into smaller, manageable tasks and set deadlines for each."**
- **"I can start by focusing on one task at a time instead of multitasking."**

Then, you take immediate action:

- You get a planner and start writing down your to-dos.
- You break a big project into smaller chunks and set up a timeline.
- You put away your phone and focus on one task at a time.

By switching from **Why?** to **What?**, you start to build momentum and **take control** of your situation. Instead of spinning in circles, you're actively improving your approach and making progress.

Concrete Examples:

Let's dive into some practical examples of how to turn **Why?** questions into **What?** questions, and how you can take action from there.

Example 1: Why Am I Stupid?

- **Why question:** *"Why am I stupid? I keep making the same mistakes."*
- **What question:** *"What do I need to learn from this situation?"*
- **Clarification:** *"I need to learn how to handle pressure better and avoid rushing through tasks."*
- **Action:** *Take a course on stress management or practice mindfulness to improve focus. Slow down and review your work before finishing.*

This shift from self-criticism to problem-solving helps you focus on what can be done differently, rather than getting stuck in negative self-talk. By slowing down and reviewing your work carefully, you'll avoid rushing and reduce the likelihood of making mistakes under pressure.

Example 2: Why Do I Keep Failing?

- **Why question:** *"Why do I keep failing? I'm just not good at anything."*
- **What question:** *"What can I do differently next time?"*
- **Clarification:** *"Next time, I'll break the task down into smaller steps*

and ask for feedback during the process."
- **Action:** *Reframe your approach by setting small, achievable goals and seeking feedback early on to adjust your course of action.*

Instead of internalizing failure, you focus on **actionable changes** you can make. By breaking tasks into smaller, manageable pieces and getting feedback along the way, you can build confidence and increase your chances of success. This proactive approach leads to growth, not more self-blame.

Example 3: Why Am I So Lazy?

- **Why question:** *"Why am I so lazy? I can't seem to get anything done."*
- **What question:** *"What action can I take right now to make progress?"*
- **Clarification:** *"I can start by tackling the most important task for the next 15 minutes."*
- **Action:** *Set a timer for 15 minutes and focus solely on that task. After 15 minutes, take a break, then go again.*

Instead of labeling yourself as "lazy," you focus on **taking immediate action**. The 15-minute timer creates a manageable time frame, helping you overcome procrastination and get started. Once you make progress, you'll feel a sense of accomplishment, which will motivate you to continue.

Why "What?" Works

The difference between a **productive** question and an **unproductive** question lies in how they guide your thinking and behavior. When you ask the right kinds of questions, you direct your energy toward **solutions** and **action**. When you ask the wrong questions, you stay stuck in confusion, guilt, or helplessness. That's why the **What?** question is so effective: it shifts you from being passive and overwhelmed to being active and empowered.

The Problem with "Why?" Questions

Ask yourself: when you're caught up in a **Why?** question, where does it take you?

- **"Why am I so stupid?"**
- **"Why do I always fail?"**

- **"Why can't I get anything right?"**

These types of questions trap you in the **past**. They keep you circling around your mistakes, your perceived shortcomings, and your failures. But where does that lead you?

- More **self-criticism**.
- More **guilt**.
- More **blame**.

What do you gain? Absolutely nothing that helps you move forward. Instead, you end up burdened by negative emotions and a sense of **powerlessness**.

The fundamental issue with **Why?** questions is that they focus on things you **can't control or change**. You can't change the past, and you can't erase your mistakes. So when you ask "Why?", you're inviting yourself to get stuck in a cycle of blame and shame. This keeps you grounded in your negative feelings instead of **moving toward solutions**.

In essence, **Why?** questions don't move you forward—they drag you deeper into a **mental and emotional hole**.

The Problem with "How?" Questions

Now, let's talk about **How?** questions. While they aren't as destructive as **Why?**, they can still be problematic, especially when they're too broad.

Consider these examples:

- **"How do I fix this?"**
- **"How do I make everything better?"**
- **"How do I get my life together?"**

These questions sound like they should be helpful, right? But the problem is, they are often so **vague** and **overwhelming** that they paralyze you instead of motivating you.

- **"How do I fix this?"** – Fixing what? How do you tackle a huge problem with no clear starting point?

- **"How do I make everything better?"** – "Everything"? That's a lot to handle. Where do you even begin?
- **"How do I get my life together?"** – This one is so broad that it can leave you feeling lost and unsure of where to start.

The **How?** question, when it's too broad, introduces **analysis paralysis**. You might think that you need to have a comprehensive plan for everything, which makes you freeze up. Instead of solving a problem, you're left thinking about the **end goal**—which often feels unattainable—and getting overwhelmed.

Why "What?" Questions Work

In contrast to **Why?** and **How?** questions, **What?** questions are **focused**, **actionable**, and **solution-oriented**. When you ask a **What?** question, you're seeking answers that can **move you forward**. They invite you to think about **practical steps** you can take right now.

Let's look at how **What?** questions help:

- **What do I need to learn from this?**
- **What can I do differently next time?**
- **What action can I take right now?**

These are questions that allow you to **move forward** because they don't keep you stuck in the past or frozen by complexity. They prompt you to find immediate solutions and take action. The focus shifts from **analyzing the problem** to **solving the problem**, which gives you a sense of control and momentum.

Why Does This Matter?

When you ask **What?** questions, you open up the **possibility of growth**. You stop feeling overwhelmed by the enormity of your problems and instead start taking clear, manageable steps toward improvement. You shift from being a passive thinker to an active problem-solver. This is how change happens.

In a nutshell, **What?** questions:

- **Clarify** the situation.
- **Generate** actionable answers.

- **Encourage** you to take the next step.

Instead of sinking into confusion, frustration, or guilt, you're putting your energy into **solving problems** and **moving forward**.

The Problem with "What If ?" Questions

You might think that asking **"What if ?"** questions is a good way to explore possibilities or prepare for different outcomes, but they can often lead you into a mental trap. Here's why:

They Lead to Unnecessary Worry

"What if?" questions tend to be **future-oriented** and often focus on **worst-case scenarios**. They can trigger anxiety, as your mind spirals into all the potential negative outcomes that might never even happen. For example:

- **"What if I fail?"**
- **"What if I embarrass myself ?"**
- **"What if they don't like me?"**

These questions create unnecessary fear and doubt, distracting you from the present moment. They focus on hypothetical situations that are often based on fear rather than reality. Instead of acting in the present, you end up paralyzed by future fears that may never come to fruition.

They Don't Help You Solve Problems

"What if?" questions often don't offer solutions. They may open up a world of possible outcomes, but they don't give you a clear path forward. They leave you thinking about all the potential **"what-ifs"** without narrowing your focus on **what needs to be done now**. For example:

- **"What if I don't get the job?"**
- **"What if I miss the deadline?"**
- **"What if I make a mistake?"**

These questions can leave you feeling stuck, unsure of what steps to take, because they don't generate specific, actionable solutions. Instead of tackling a real challenge, you're lost in **what could happen**, not **what is happening**.

They Are Based on Assumptions, Not Reality

Often, the scenarios you imagine in response to "What if?" questions are exaggerated or **based on assumptions** rather than facts. You can easily imagine an extreme outcome (e.g., **"What if they fire me?"**) when the reality is usually much more measured (e.g., **"I can learn from my mistakes and improve my performance"**).

This tendency to focus on the worst-case scenario distorts your perception and creates unnecessary stress. Instead of examining the situation realistically and calmly, you're adding unnecessary complexity and fear to the equation.

How to Shift from "What If?" to "What?"

Instead of spiraling into hypothetical worst-case scenarios with "What if?" questions, reframe them into "What?" questions. This shift brings you back to **action** and **clarity**.

Here's how to do it:

- **Instead of "What if I fail?" ask "What can I do to succeed?"**
  - Shift your focus to **preparing** and **taking action** instead of worrying about the possibility of failure.
- **Instead of "What if they don't like me?" ask "What can I do to be authentic and engage with them?"**
  - Focus on **connection, genuine interaction**, and **bringing your best self forward** rather than imagining rejection.
- **Instead of "What if I make a mistake?" ask "What can I learn from mistakes to improve next time?"**
  - Shift your focus from avoiding mistakes to seeing them as **learning opportunities** for growth.

Why This Works:

- **Shifting from "What if?" to "What?"** helps you regain control over the situation, turning your attention to what you can actually **influence** and **do**.
- "What?" questions ground you in the **present** and help you focus on what **actionable steps** you can take.
- You start thinking in terms of solutions, rather than getting stuck in

fear, uncertainty, or hypothetical scenarios that are out of your control.

"What if?" questions can lead you into anxiety, overwhelm, and indecision, whereas **"What?"** questions are practical, solution-focused, and actionable. When you replace "What if?" with "What?" you move from **fear** to **empowerment**, from **confusion** to **clarity**, and from **inaction** to **progress**.

How to Use the "What?" Activity

The **What? Activity** is a straightforward process for transforming negative, intrusive thoughts into actionable steps. Here's how you can apply it:

Identify the Intrusive Thought

Start by recognizing any recurring thought that causes stress, discomfort, or frustration. These are the thoughts that you'll target using the **What? Activity**.

Examples:

- "Why am I so overweight?"
- "Why do I always mess up?"
- "Why can't I get anything right?"

These types of questions are often self-critical and leave you feeling stuck. The key here is to acknowledge the thought without judgment. Once you've identified the thought, you can move to the next step.

Reframe the Thought with "What?"

Rather than staying stuck in negative self-blame or guilt, shift the question to something more constructive using **What?**. This reframes the focus from what went wrong or why it happened to what you can do to improve the situation.

Examples:

- "What can I do to lose weight?"
- "What can I do to stop making these mistakes?"
- "What steps can I take to improve my skills?"

Why it works: This shift from **Why?** to **What?** helps you take control. Instead of spiraling in self-criticism, you start focusing on potential solutions and actions.

Brainstorm Actionable Options

Now that you've reframed your thought, the next step is to brainstorm possible actions you can take to address the issue. Let your mind generate a list of options—no matter how small or big. The **What?** question prompts your brain to think about ways to improve the situation instead of wallowing in negativity.

Examples for Weight Loss:

- I can track my calorie intake.
- I can start exercising for 20 minutes a day.
- I can research nutrition plans or consult with a dietitian.

Examples for Stopping Mistakes:

- I can break my tasks into smaller, manageable chunks.
- I can practice mindfulness techniques to stay focused.
- I can learn new skills through online courses or seek feedback from a mentor.

The idea here is to generate a variety of possible solutions, which empowers you by showing that there are many ways to tackle the problem, rather than getting bogged down by the issue itself.

Choose the Best Option and Dive In

Once you've brainstormed your options, choose the one that seems the most feasible, appealing, or urgent. If you're not sure which direction to take, you can ask another **What?** question to gain more clarity.

Examples for Weight Loss:

- "What do I need to do first to manage my calorie intake?"
  - I can look up healthy food choices online.
  - I can consult a nutritionist for personalized advice.
  - I can start by reducing sugar and processed foods.

Examples for Stopping Mistakes:

- "What's the first thing I can do today to focus better?"
    - I can break my work into smaller, more manageable steps.
    - I can create a checklist for my tasks today.
    - I can set a timer to avoid distractions during tasks.

By being specific, you create a clear first step and make it easier to take action. If you feel stuck after identifying a step, just ask another **What?** to clarify further.

Take Action

Action is the most crucial part of the process. This is where you start implementing the steps you've identified. The more you act on your insights, the faster you'll break free from the negative thought cycle and begin to build momentum toward positive change.

Examples:

- If your first step for weight loss is to research healthy foods, set aside time today to search for nutritional information or reach out to a nutritionist for advice.
- If your first step for improving focus is to create a checklist, do it now, even if it's just a short list of tasks for today. Write it down, and commit to following it.

Taking immediate action reinforces your ability to control the situation, shifting your focus from what you can't control to what you **can** do now.

Recap of Steps:

- **Identify the Intrusive Thought:** Recognize the negative thought that's causing stress.
- **Reframe the Thought with "What?":** Shift the question from "Why?" to "What?" to focus on solutions.
- **Brainstorm Actionable Options:** List practical steps you can take to address the issue.
- **Choose the Best Option and Dive In:** Select the most feasible step

and clarify the first action.

- **Take Action:** Implement the chosen action right away.

The **What? Activity** is a simple but effective tool to shift from negative thinking to positive action. By practicing this method consistently, you'll start transforming your mindset from feeling stuck to taking control and moving forward.

More Scenarios for the "What?" Activity

Here are some additional example scenarios to illustrate how to apply the **What? Activity** in various situations:

Thought: "I feel stuck in my career."

- **Reframe with What?:**
  What can I do to feel more fulfilled at work?
- **Brainstorm Actionable Options:**
  - Explore new responsibilities or projects within your current role.
  - Seek out networking opportunities within your industry.
  - Take an online course to develop new skills or certifications.
  - Consider talking to a career coach for personalized advice.
- **Choose the Best Option:**
  Choose one option, like **researching career development opportunities** or **signing up for a professional development workshop**, and begin with small steps, such as reviewing potential courses or networking events.

Thought: "I never have enough time."

- **Reframe with What?:**
  What can I do to manage my time better?
- **Brainstorm Actionable Options:**
  - Prioritize your tasks by urgency and importance.
  - Delegate tasks that can be handled by others.
  - Set clear boundaries by saying no to non-essential commitments.

- ° Simplify your daily schedule by cutting out time-wasting activities or distractions.
- **Choose the Best Option**:
  Select the most effective option, such as **creating a daily schedule** that prioritizes important tasks, or **using a time-blocking technique** to dedicate focus time for deep work.

Thought: "I'm always anxious about social situations."

- **Reframe with What?**:
  What can I do to reduce my social anxiety?
- **Brainstorm Actionable Options**:
  - ° Practice **deep breathing exercises** to calm your nerves before social events.
  - ° Prepare conversation topics or questions in advance to feel more confident.
  - ° Consider **seeking support from a therapist** or coach for anxiety management strategies.
  - ° Start small with **attending smaller social events** and gradually work your way up to larger gatherings.
- **Choose the Best Option**:
  Start with one small action, such as **practicing deep breathing exercises** before a social event or **attending a smaller gathering** to ease into more complex social situations.

Thought: "I always procrastinate and never get things done."

- **Reframe with What?**:
  What can I do to overcome procrastination?
- **Brainstorm Actionable Options**:
  - ° Break tasks down into smaller, manageable steps.
  - ° Set a **timer** for focused work sessions (like Pomodoro Technique).
  - ° Remove distractions by turning off notifications or working in a quiet environment.
  - ° Set clear **deadlines** and hold yourself accountable.

- **Choose the Best Option**:
  Pick one action to implement today, such as **setting a 25-minute timer** for focused work or **breaking a large project** into smaller, more actionable tasks.

Thought: "I'm not good enough to succeed."

- **Reframe with What?**:
  What can I do to improve my skills or confidence?
- **Brainstorm Actionable Options**:
  - Take **small steps to improve** your skills—start with a workshop, online course, or book.
  - Practice **positive self-talk** and affirmations.
  - Seek **feedback** from a mentor or colleague to gain constructive insights.
  - Reflect on your **previous successes** to remind yourself of your capabilities.
- **Choose the Best Option**:
  Select one practical step, like **setting up a meeting with a mentor** or **signing up for a course** to work on improving a specific skill.

Thought: "I feel overwhelmed by everything I need to do."

- **Reframe with What?**:
  What can I do to manage my overwhelm?
- **Brainstorm Actionable Options**:
  - **Prioritize** the most important tasks and tackle them first.
  - Break large tasks into **smaller, more manageable steps**.
  - **Delegate** tasks where possible, or ask for help.
  - Set realistic expectations by acknowledging what you can **reasonably accomplish** in a given time frame.
- **Choose the Best Option**:
  Pick one immediate action, like **writing a to-do list and prioritizing tasks** based on deadlines or importance. You can also **take a few minutes to meditate** to clear your mind before tackling the first task.

Thought: "I never get along with my coworkers."

- **Reframe with What?:**
  What can I do to improve my relationship with my coworkers?
- **Brainstorm Actionable Options:**
    - Take the initiative to **start conversations** and get to know them better.
    - **Listen actively** and offer help when appropriate to build rapport.
    - Set boundaries for healthy communication and conflict resolution.
    - Seek feedback from coworkers or managers on how to improve your work relationships.
- **Choose the Best Option:**
  Choose one action, like **reaching out for a casual chat** with a colleague or **asking for feedback** on your interactions to improve communication.

Thought: "I'm always tired and never have energy."

- **Reframe with What?:**
  What can I do to feel more energized?
- **Brainstorm Actionable Options:**
    - **Improve your sleep hygiene** by establishing a bedtime routine.
    - Increase your **physical activity** with regular exercise.
    - Eat a balanced, **nutritious diet** to fuel your body.
    - **Manage stress** with relaxation techniques such as meditation or journaling.
- **Choose the Best Option:**
  Start with one practical step, like **setting a consistent sleep schedule** or **committing to a 15-minute walk** each day to boost energy.

Thought: "I can't handle this new project."

- **Reframe with What?:**
  What can I do to manage this project effectively?
- **Brainstorm Actionable Options:**

- ○ Break the project down into smaller, **manageable tasks**.
- ○ **Set clear deadlines** for each task and work backwards to stay on track.
- ○ Reach out to a **mentor or colleague** for advice on how to approach the project.
- ○ **Delegate** tasks where possible or ask for help when needed.
- **Choose the Best Option**:
  Choose one step, such as **breaking the project down into stages** or **setting a meeting with a colleague** to discuss priorities and timeline.

Thought: "I keep making the same mistake over and over."

- **Reframe with What?**:
  What can I learn from this mistake?
- **Brainstorm Actionable Options**:
  - ○ Identify the **root cause** of the mistake and create strategies to avoid repeating it.
  - ○ **Seek feedback** from others to get an outside perspective.
  - ○ Implement a **self-review process** before completing tasks to catch errors early.
  - ○ Practice **mindfulness** or **focus techniques** to stay present and avoid hasty decisions.
- **Choose the Best Option**:
  Select a specific action, like **asking a colleague for feedback** or **creating a checklist** to review your work before submission.

By consistently applying the **What? Activity**, you begin to shift your mindset from feeling stuck and overwhelmed to feeling empowered and capable. The beauty of this method is its simplicity—ask **What?**, break down your problems into actionable steps, and take control of the situation.

Why This Works: The Power of Action

The **What? Activity** isn't just about asking better questions; it's about taking action. It's about regaining control of your thoughts and shifting from a passive, stuck state to one of empowerment and clarity. When you engage with a What? question, you're actively breaking the cycle of overthinking, self-doubt, and paralysis.

Here's the key: Thoughts can often feel like a heavy fog, clouding your judgment and making everything seem more confusing and overwhelming than it is. When you're trapped in negative thinking, it's easy to get pulled into a cycle of self-blame and indecision. Thoughts like *"Why am I so stuck?"* or *"Why can't I get anything right?"* only feed that cycle, making the fog thicker.

But when you shift to **What?**, you cut through that fog. You break free from the endless loops of rumination and move into action. You move from a state of confusion to clarity. Instead of asking questions that leave you trapped in self-judgment, like *"Why am I failing?"* you ask, *"What can I learn from this?"* That shift instantly refocuses your mind on potential solutions.

The power of **What?** is that it changes your mindset from victimhood and frustration to action and empowerment. You no longer stay stuck in the past or overwhelmed by uncertainty. You create a path forward.

The **What? Activity** interrupts the spiral of overthinking and doubt. It forces you to pause, reframe, and act. By making this shift, you're stepping out of the mental fog and into the driver's seat of your own life.

This is why it works: action leads to change. When you stop ruminating and start doing, you begin to break free from the mental loops that have held you back. You stop waiting for the right moment or for things to feel perfect, and instead, you take the next step—no matter how small it may seem. And with every step you take, you build momentum toward real, lasting change.

When you ask **What?**, you're not just asking a question—you're deciding to do something about it. You're choosing to clear the fog, take action, and create a path toward progress. This simple shift in how you think and act is what makes all the difference.

A Complementary Approach to Personal Growth

The beauty of the **What? Activity** lies in its ability to complement other growth strategies, creating a powerful, integrated approach to personal development. It doesn't exist in isolation. Instead, it works seamlessly with other techniques—most notably, the **Perfect Thought Activity**.

Think of the **Perfect Thought Activity** as your foundational tool for neutralizing negative thoughts. It helps you detach from the emotional charge of destructive, self-limiting beliefs. The key here is that it helps you *recognize* negative thoughts without getting swept away by them. You acknowledge their presence, but they no longer have control over your actions. However, as we all know, those negative thoughts can sometimes be persistent. When the negative self-talk starts to creep back in, that's where the **What? Activity** steps in.

While the **Perfect Thought Activity** helps you regain emotional distance from your thoughts, the **What? Activity** provides a next step. It shifts you from rehashing negative emotions to taking proactive steps that will move you forward. Instead of cycling through guilt, frustration, or confusion, you shift your focus toward actionable solutions.

But that's not all. The **What? Activity** also connects with the **Perfect Moment Activity**, which encourages staying grounded in the present. When you're using **What?** questions, you're pulling yourself out of the past—where "Why?" questions often trap you—and pushing yourself toward practical, present-moment actions. It helps you stay anchored in the here and now, so you're not weighed down by past mistakes or paralyzed by future uncertainties.

By connecting these activities, you build a holistic approach to personal growth. The **Perfect Thought Activity** helps you detach and neutralize negative thinking, the **What? Activity** empowers you to take action, and the **Perfect Moment Activity** ensures you're always focused on what you can do right now. Together, these techniques give you the tools to break free from the cycles that hold you back and move forward with clarity and purpose.

From Thought to Action: The Shift

The true power of the **What? Activity** lies in its ability to transform mental energy into action. It's not about getting bogged down in why things aren't working or rehashing what's gone wrong. Instead, it's about shifting your focus to what you can do to make things work. It's a shift from confusion to clarity, from overthinking to doing.

Whenever you find yourself stuck in a spiral of negative thoughts or frustration—when you're endlessly wondering, "Why am I so bad at this?" or "Why can't I get it right?"—replace that **Why?** with a **What?**. Ask yourself, "What can I do to improve this situation?" or "What's the next step I can take?" That simple switch opens up a world of actionable possibilities and immediately puts you in the driver's seat.

The beauty of the **What? Activity** is that the more you practice it, the more natural it becomes to turn any troubling thought or obstacle into a practical solution. Over time, you stop getting lost in mental loops. Instead, you start shifting into action faster, moving from uncertainty to tangible steps without getting stuck in analysis paralysis.

By consistently using the **What? Activity**, you condition yourself to approach challenges with clarity, decisiveness, and confidence. You stop allowing your thoughts to overwhelm or paralyze you and begin transforming those thoughts into productive actions. And the more you do this, the less time you'll spend stuck in your head—and the more you'll see real progress in your life.

Let Me Say It Again: Ask "What?" Not "Why?"

When you're grappling with negative or troubling thoughts, the instinct is often to ask **"Why?"** But here's the truth: **Why?** doesn't lead you to solutions. It doesn't propel you forward. It keeps you stuck in mental loops of confusion, self-doubt, and emotional reaction. Instead, **"What?"** is the question that moves you toward clarity, action, and practical solutions.

Here's Why "What?" Works Better Than "Why?"

"Why?" Traps You in Stories and Excuses

When you ask **"Why?"**, you're often asking yourself to justify, explain, or rationalize your situation, which leads to endless stories. Think about how many times you've asked yourself:

- *"Why do I feel so anxious?"*
- *"Why do I keep making the same mistakes?"*

If you dig deep enough, your mind will generate reasons and justifications that only fuel the cycle of self-doubt, guilt, or victimhood.

Example:

- **Why do I feel stuck in my career?**
    - This question might lead you to stories like: *"I'm not talented enough," "I didn't get the right opportunities,"* or *"My boss doesn't like me."*
    - These explanations don't help. They reinforce the belief that you're powerless or that the situation is beyond your control.

"What?" Leads to Actionable Insights

In contrast, **"What?"** shifts the focus from justifying the problem to finding a solution. It moves you from self-pity to action, from analysis paralysis to clarity. Asking **"What?"** empowers you to break free from the mental fog and make clear, specific decisions.

Example:

- **What can I do to move forward in my career?**
  - This question directs your brain to focus on practical steps: *"I can seek additional training," "I can network with people in my field,"* or *"I can speak to a career coach for guidance."*
  - Now you have a tangible, actionable plan rather than getting stuck in unproductive thoughts.

"Why?" Keeps You Focused on the Past

"Why?" often keeps you stuck in the past, dissecting old mistakes or things you cannot change. Focusing on causes that are out of your control triggers frustration, shame, or hopelessness.

Example:

- **Why did I fail last time?**
  - This question pulls you into a cycle of past failure, which makes it harder to break free from feelings of defeat. Instead of learning from mistakes, you stay emotionally attached to them, preventing forward movement.

"What?" Puts You in the Present and Future

On the other hand, **"What?"** pulls you into the present moment and points you toward the future. It shifts the focus to what you can do now and what steps you can take moving forward, helping you stay grounded in the present, where your power lies.

Example:

- **What can I do right now to improve my health?**
  - This question focuses on actionable steps: *"I can go for a walk," "I can eat a healthier meal,"* or *"I can schedule a checkup."*

- You're no longer bogged down by the past, and you're actively focused on what you can do today.

"Why?" Can Lead to Circular Thinking

Asking **"Why?"** can make you go in circles without ever really getting anywhere. It encourages overthinking, which can lead to confusion, self-doubt, and frustration. You can waste hours, days, or even years wondering **why** something happened or **why** you are the way you are without ever finding a clear solution.

Example:

- **Why am I always so tired?**
    - This question could lead to an endless loop of self-analysis: *"Maybe it's my diet, maybe it's stress, maybe it's lack of sleep..."*
    - But it doesn't point you to a concrete action.

Solution: Ask "What can I do to improve my energy levels?"

- Now, you're asking your mind to focus on actionable solutions: *"I could improve my sleep hygiene," "I could eat more balanced meals,"* or *"I could set a morning routine."*

"What?" Prompts You to Take Responsibility and Action

A key advantage of asking **"What?"** is that it immediately places you in a position of personal responsibility. Instead of blaming others or external circumstances, you're looking for practical solutions that are within your control.

Example:

- **What can I do to stop procrastinating?**
    - This question encourages you to think about actions you can take: *"I can break down tasks into smaller steps," "I can set clearer goals,"* or *"I can use a timer to manage my time."*
    - You're empowered to take action, and you realize you have the ability to change the situation.

"Why?" Often Triggers Emotions That Can Derail Progress

"**Why?**" questions often stir up emotional reactions that can derail progress. If you ask "**Why am I so anxious?**" or "**Why do I always mess up?**" your emotions may escalate, reinforcing negative thought patterns. This emotional spiral can drain your energy and leave you feeling even more stuck.

Example:

- **Why is everything so overwhelming?**
    - This question might generate panic, stress, or hopelessness, making it harder to take action.

Solution: Ask "**What can I do to manage my stress right now?**"

- Now you're focused on specific, practical steps like: *"I can take a few deep breaths," "I can organize my tasks for the day,"* or *"I can talk to a friend for support."*
- You immediately shift from emotional overwhelm to actionable clarity.

The Bottom Line: Shift from "Why?" to "What?"

Asking "**What?**" doesn't just change the question—it changes the entire game. Instead of staying stuck in confusion, blame, or reactivity, you move into clarity, empowerment, and action.

You stop overanalyzing and justifying the past. You stop circling in your head about what went wrong. Instead, you focus on **what you can do to move forward.**

So, the next time you find yourself questioning your thoughts or feeling stuck, don't get bogged down by the past. Ask yourself, "**What can I do now?**" and watch how quickly you shift from uncertainty to action.

This is the key to unlocking the power of momentum. What? opens the door to transformation—one deliberate step at a time.

Key Takeaways:

- **Stop asking "Why?" questions**: They lead to self-criticism, guilt, and emotional loops, keeping you stuck in a cycle of blame without offering solutions.

- **Start asking "What?" questions**: These questions direct your focus toward actionable solutions, empowering you to take control and move forward.
- **Clarify your "What?" questions**: The more specific you are, the more precise your answers will be. Clear, actionable questions lead to clear, actionable solutions.
- **Act on the answers immediately**: Don't overthink or stay stuck in analysis. Once you have clarity, take action. The more you act, the more progress you'll make.

The What? Activity: A Mindset Shift

The **What? Activity** transforms you from a passive thinker into an active problem-solver. It cuts through mental clutter, helps you refocus your energy, and puts you back in the driver's seat of your life. With regular practice, you'll develop a stronger, more resilient mindset that empowers you to handle challenges with clarity and confidence.

- **Breaks the cycle of overthinking**: Shifts you from confusion to action.
- **Focuses on solutions**: Stops you from getting stuck in self-doubt or blame.
- **Promotes forward momentum**: Moves you toward actionable steps, while "Why?" keeps you trapped in the past.
- **Holistic approach**: Combines with the **Perfect Thought** and **Perfect Moment Activities**, creating a comprehensive method for shifting your mindset and achieving your goals.

Your Next Step

The next time a troubling thought arises, **don't get trapped in "Why?"** Instead, ask **"What?"** and watch how quickly you start moving from thought to action.

The **What? Activity** works because it shifts you out of a victim mindset and into the role of a proactive problem-solver. It replaces helplessness with empowerment.

- **Recognize** when you're stuck in the negative loop of "Why?" and interrupt it with "What?"
- **Shift your focus** from the problem to the solution.
- **Clarify** your "What?" question to make the solution specific and actionable.
- **Act** on the answers and create real, tangible progress.

By consistently practicing the **What? Activity**, you'll break free from endless self-doubt and begin taking proactive steps to move forward.

Perfect Thought Extension: The Perfect Moment

Expanding the Perfect Thought Activity to the Perfect Moment Activity

The **Perfect Thought Activity** has already revolutionized how you approach your internal dialogue. But what if you could take that same powerful approach and apply it to every moment of your life—not just your thoughts, but the actual experiences you go through? Instead of reacting with frustration, resistance, or judgment, what if you could look at every moment and say, **"This moment is perfect now?"**

That's where the **Perfect Moment Activity** comes in.

The core idea behind the **Perfect Moment Activity** is simple, yet incredibly powerful: it's about embracing the present moment—no matter what it contains—with full acceptance. It's about recognizing that whatever is happening **right now**, whether it's something you want or something you'd rather avoid, is exactly as it needs to be. There's no resistance. No judgment. Just acceptance.

Why the Perfect Moment Works

In our everyday lives, we tend to spend a lot of time fighting against what's happening in the present. We wish things were different, that we could change something, or we resist accepting what's in front of us. But what if, instead of trying to control every detail, we decided to simply accept the moment as it is? By doing so, we release the mental and emotional strain of judgment, and we stop resisting the current reality. We create a harmony between ourselves and the world around us, rather than constantly battling it.

How the Perfect Moment Activity Works

Imagine this scenario:

You're running late for an appointment. Traffic is a nightmare. Your phone dies. You're watching the clock tick away. You have two choices in this moment:

- **Choice 1**: You get frustrated, angry, and annoyed by the situation. You think about how unfair it is, how everything is going wrong, and how things are working against you. You spiral into frustration, which only adds more tension and stress to the moment.
- **Choice 2**: You take a deep breath and say to yourself, **"This moment**

is perfect now."

This doesn't mean you stop trying to get to your appointment or that you passively accept the situation. Instead, it means you accept where you are right now, without judgment. You recognize that this moment, as imperfect as it may seem, is exactly as it needs to be. Instead of fighting reality, you choose to flow with it.

The Impact of This Shift

By choosing to embrace the moment with acceptance, you release the mental energy that would otherwise go toward frustration, worry, or resistance. This shift allows you to let go of emotional burdens and unnecessary stress. As a result, you can move forward with a clear, calm mind, focused on what needs to be done rather than being bogged down by negative emotions or self-blame.

You stop **fighting** the moment and start **working with** it. This makes your actions more effective, as you're not overwhelmed by negative thoughts or emotions. You're able to make decisions from a place of clarity, rather than being clouded by frustration or resistance.

The Benefits of the Perfect Moment Activity

- **Reduces Stress and Anxiety**: By accepting the present moment, you stop feeding negative emotional reactions. Instead of dwelling on what's wrong, you focus on what you can do with the situation at hand.
- **Improves Focus**: When you stop resisting and start accepting, you clear your mind of distractions, making it easier to focus on what needs to be done.
- **Promotes Inner Peace**: The act of embracing the moment as perfect brings a sense of calm and harmony with reality. It encourages you to stop battling life and instead, embrace it with open arms.
- **Enhances Problem-Solving**: Acceptance doesn't mean complacency. It means being present and aware, which actually helps you see clearer solutions and make more effective decisions.

A Practical Example

You're facing a difficult situation at work, perhaps an overwhelming project with tight deadlines. Your first instinct might be to feel stressed and question how you're going to get it all done. However, instead of going down that road, you practice the **Perfect Moment Activity**:

- **You say to yourself**: "This moment is perfect now. I am here, and this is exactly where I need to be."
- You accept the reality of the situation as it is, without judgment or self-criticism. You acknowledge that the challenge you're facing is part of your growth.
- From this space of calm acceptance, you can look at the task with a clear mind and make decisions on how to prioritize and break it down into manageable steps.

By doing this, you transform an otherwise stressful moment into one of clarity and action, rather than getting trapped in overwhelm and resistance.

Integrating the Perfect Moment with the Perfect Thought Activity

The **Perfect Moment Activity** is a natural extension of the **Perfect Thought Activity**. While the Perfect Thought Activity helps you neutralize and transform negative thoughts into more empowering ones, the Perfect Moment Activity helps you do the same with your real-life experiences. By practicing these two activities together, you not only shift how you think but also how you experience every moment.

- The **Perfect Thought Activity** allows you to change your inner dialogue and reframe limiting beliefs.
- The **Perfect Moment Activity** enables you to embrace life as it unfolds, accepting both the challenges and the joys with full awareness and peace.

Together, they create a powerful combination for living with more presence, peace, and purpose. Instead of reacting to life with frustration or resistance, you start engaging with it in a way that brings clarity, action, and a deep sense of satisfaction.

So, the next time you find yourself faced with a difficult moment, remember: **This moment is perfect now.** Accept it, embrace it, and move forward with calm determination.

Scenario: You're stuck in traffic.

You're late for an important meeting. The minutes are ticking away. Your mind races:

- "I'm going to be late!"
- "Why is this always happening to me?"
- "This is such a waste of time!"

You can feel the frustration building. The situation is beyond your control, yet your mind begins to amplify it, creating a sense of panic and irritation.

Here's where the Perfect Moment Activity steps in.

Instead of getting lost in frustration and self-blame, you make a choice. You consciously decide to shift your mindset. You say:

"This moment is perfect now."

What does that mean?

It's not about loving the fact that you're stuck in traffic. It's not about saying, "I'm happy this is happening." Instead, you're **accepting the moment exactly as it is.** You're recognizing that this is your reality in this very moment. There is no point in fighting it because, at this moment, **you cannot change it.**

This is where peace begins.

By acknowledging that the situation is as it is, you stop the internal battle. You stop resisting the moment, and in doing so, you create mental and emotional space. You take away the emotional charge that could escalate your frustration. The moment becomes neutralized, and you gain **clarity.** You can now choose your response, free from emotional overwhelm.

How Acceptance Creates Space for Action

When you stop resisting what's happening, you're no longer trapped in a spiral of negative thoughts or reactions. Instead of continuing to fret about being late, you can calmly assess your situation:

- Maybe there's a way to adjust your schedule.
- Perhaps there's still time to call ahead and let someone know you'll be late.
- You might use the time to listen to an inspiring podcast or calm your mind before your meeting.

These are all **actionable steps** you can take when you stop fighting reality. Acceptance doesn't mean you sit back and do nothing—it gives you the **mental clarity** to see the next best steps and move forward with intention.

The Radical Power of Acceptance

By embracing the present moment as it is, you stop wasting energy on unnecessary emotional turmoil. You let go of judgment and open yourself to peace and freedom. This doesn't mean that you should never feel frustrated or that you can't want things to be different—it simply means that, in this moment, **you choose not to suffer** by fighting against what is happening.

In every situation, the more you practice the Perfect Moment Activity, the more you develop the ability to:

- Let go of unnecessary emotional weight.
- Stay grounded in the present.
- Respond from a place of peace and clarity, rather than reactivity or frustration.

This practice creates a space where life becomes easier to navigate—whether things are going your way or not.

The Difference Between Acceptance and Approval

It's important to clarify an essential point: **Acceptance does not mean approval**.

Acceptance is about recognizing and acknowledging reality for what it is, without adding layers of judgment or emotional resistance. Approval, on the other hand, implies liking or agreeing with something. When you accept a situation, you are **acknowledging it** as it is, without necessarily liking it.

For example, you may **accept** that you're stuck in traffic, but that doesn't mean you **approve** of the traffic jam. You don't have to like it, you don't have to condone it, but you **do have to recognize** that it is the reality of the moment.

And by recognizing it without resistance, you free yourself from additional mental and emotional turmoil.

Why Acceptance is Empowering

You might wonder: *If I accept things as they are, won't I just become complacent or passive?*

The answer is **no**. **Acceptance** is not about passivity or giving up—it's about **honestly acknowledging the reality** of the present moment without adding frustration, blame, or any other emotional charge to it.

Here's the truth: **Resistance creates suffering**.

Think about a time when you resisted something that was happening—whether it was a situation, a conversation, or your own emotions. Did resisting it make it better or easier to handle? Likely, it made it worse. The more you resisted, the more frustrated or upset you became.

Example of Resistance vs. Acceptance:

Let's say you're running late for an important meeting. The traffic is backed up, your phone has died, and you're watching the minutes slip away. Your first instinct might be to think:

- "This is unfair!"
- "Why does this always happen to me?"
- "I can't believe I'm stuck here!"

This is resistance. You are **fighting the reality** of the moment, and what happens when you resist? You get frustrated, angry, or upset. You mentally fuel the negative emotions, and in turn, you waste valuable energy.

Now, imagine you take a moment to breathe and **accept** what is happening. You acknowledge, **"This moment is perfect now"**. You don't like the situation, but you recognize that this is the reality. There's nothing you can do to change it in the moment. Instead of wasting energy resisting the traffic, you choose to **focus on what you can do now**.

- Maybe you could call ahead to let someone know you'll be late.
- Perhaps you can use the time to calm your mind or mentally prepare for the meeting.
- Maybe you could even listen to an inspiring podcast to make the best

of the situation.

This shift—moving from resistance to **acceptance**—opens up your mind to solutions and frees you from the emotional grip of frustration. You can respond in the moment, without being emotionally hijacked.

Resistance vs. Flow

When you resist the present moment, you keep **fighting** against what's happening. But when you choose **acceptance**, you shift from a place of struggle to a place of **flow**. You don't waste energy on "why is this happening?" or "this isn't fair." Instead, you stop fighting reality and start moving with it.

Acceptance isn't about giving up or resigning yourself to a bad situation—it's about **flowing with the current of life**, no matter what it brings. The moment may not be ideal, but by accepting it, you can be more centered, more clear-headed, and better equipped to respond to it.

The Power of Acceptance

When you accept the present moment, you release the mental and emotional burden of **resistance**. This creates space for peace, clarity, and empowerment. Instead of focusing on what you don't want to happen or wishing things were different, you can focus on what **you can do** in this moment.

Acceptance gives you the power to:

- **Let go of unnecessary emotional strain**: By acknowledging the moment, you stop struggling against it, and release frustration, anger, or worry.
- **Gain mental clarity**: Without resistance clouding your mind, you can think clearly and take practical action.
- **Respond from a place of calm**: Instead of reacting impulsively or emotionally, you can make clear, rational decisions in any situation.
- **Focus on what's within your control**: Once you accept what's happening, you stop wasting energy on what you can't change and focus on what you **can** control in the moment.

The Truth About Resistance

Here's the ultimate truth: **The moment is happening** whether you like it or not.

- If you resist it, you're only prolonging your suffering.
- If you accept it, you cut through resistance and open yourself up to peace, clarity, and proactive action.

Resistance holds you **back**. Acceptance allows you to move **forward**—even when things are challenging. It enables you to stop wasting time and emotional energy fighting against the moment, and instead, focus on how you can respond **effectively**.

Additional Real-Life Examples of Acceptance:

- **Dealing with Unexpected Changes at Work:** You've spent days preparing for an important presentation, only to be told at the last minute that the meeting has been rescheduled. Your immediate reaction might be frustration or even panic—thinking to yourself, "This is so unfair! Why do things keep changing on me?" Instead of spiraling, stop for a moment and breathe. **Accept the situation** as it is. You don't have control over the schedule changes, but you can control your response.
  Shift your perspective: "This moment is perfect now." You now have an opportunity to reframe your thinking. Maybe you use the extra time to refine your presentation or relax your mind before you present later. You choose to make the best of the situation, using the unexpected change to your advantage. Acceptance releases the emotional weight of frustration and opens up space for creative solutions.
- **Managing a Difficult Conversation with a Loved One:** You're in a conversation with a friend or partner, and tensions are rising. You feel defensive, angry, or misunderstood. You want to argue, explain, or prove your point.
  Pause. Before reacting, say to yourself: "This moment is perfect now." **Acceptance** in this case means acknowledging the emotion, acknowledging the conversation, and stepping out of the heat of the

moment. You may not like what's being said, but you can choose to accept the present moment and how you're feeling. This clarity allows you to respond from a place of calm rather than reacting emotionally. You might say something like, "I'm feeling upset, and I need a moment to collect my thoughts," which helps de-escalate the situation and brings you back to a place of mutual understanding.

- **Experiencing a Health Setback:** After months of training for a marathon, you sustain an injury that prevents you from running. Initially, you may feel frustrated, defeated, or discouraged—thoughts like, "Why did this happen to me now? I've worked so hard!" can flood your mind.

  Acceptance doesn't mean giving up on your goal. It means **accepting the reality of the moment** without unnecessary emotional drama. Say to yourself: "This moment is perfect now." You acknowledge the injury and your frustration, but you let go of any resistance. Instead of obsessing over what you can't control, you focus on what you **can** control: perhaps focusing on rehab, cross-training, or learning more about your body's needs. By accepting this setback, you free yourself from emotional suffering and allow yourself to find a path forward that works within the current circumstances.

- **Facing a Financial Setback:** You receive an unexpected expense, like a car repair bill or a medical emergency, that throws off your budget for the month. It's easy to get angry or overwhelmed, thinking, "Why does this always happen? This is such bad luck!"
  Instead, practice **acceptance** by taking a moment to acknowledge that the situation is frustrating, but it is what it is right now.
  Shift your focus: "This moment is perfect now." Instead of sinking into worry or shame, you recognize that there's nothing to be gained from resisting the present moment. You can now look at your finances with clarity, maybe prioritize expenses or even reach out for advice. Acceptance allows you to make decisions from a place of calm and empowerment, instead of panic or blame.

- **Stuck in a Long Line at the Store:** You're at the checkout counter, and the line is moving slower than you anticipated. You're in a rush and beginning to feel annoyed. Thoughts like "Why does this always happen?" start to flood your mind.

Stop. Breathe.

Now, apply **acceptance**. Say to yourself: "This moment is perfect now." Acknowledge that you cannot change the fact that the line is long, but you can choose how to respond.

Maybe you use the time to be more present—perhaps mentally checking off things on your to-do list or even striking up a friendly conversation with the person in front of you. By accepting the moment instead of resisting it, you turn a frustrating experience into an opportunity to practice patience and mindfulness.

- **Receiving Criticism at Work:** During a meeting, your boss provides feedback that you perceive as harsh or unfair. Your first instinct might be to react defensively or feel upset, telling yourself, "They don't understand me" or "This isn't true."

  Instead of reacting impulsively, pause. **Accept** the moment: "This moment is perfect now."

  This doesn't mean you agree with everything said, but it means you acknowledge the feedback and your emotional reaction without letting it control you. By accepting the situation, you create space for reflection. Maybe you ask for clarification or constructive ways to improve. Acceptance helps you respond with maturity and openness, rather than defensiveness or frustration.

- **Dealing with Family Drama:** A family member is upset with you, and tensions are rising. You feel yourself getting defensive or wanting to explain yourself. It's easy to feel wronged or misunderstood.

  Take a step back. **Accept the moment**: "This moment is perfect now." Accepting the situation means acknowledging that both your emotions and the other person's emotions are valid. You can pause, listen, and choose your response from a place of understanding and clarity, rather than reacting emotionally. Instead of engaging in the drama, you focus on how to move forward in a way that supports harmony and resolution.

Real-Life Example of Resistance at Work:

You're facing an overwhelming deadline at work. Your boss is expecting results, and you feel an immense amount of pressure building up. Your mind starts racing through worst-case scenarios: *What if I don't finish in time? What if I fail? What if this makes me look bad?* Your body tenses up, and your stress levels skyrocket. You start thinking that you *should* be more prepared, or that you *shouldn't* feel this way.

This resistance—telling yourself that this situation *shouldn't* be so stressful, or that you *shouldn't* feel anxious—is exactly where the suffering lies. You're adding emotional weight to a situation that, in itself, is already challenging enough.

Now, imagine taking a moment to stop resisting. You stop battling against the stress and say to yourself:

"This moment is perfect now."

This doesn't mean you stop caring about the deadline or give up on doing your best. It simply means you stop adding unnecessary layers of frustration or anxiety. You accept the reality of the moment, including the stress, and give yourself permission to deal with it as it is. This mental shift frees you from unnecessary emotional turmoil, allowing you to focus on what needs to be done without the extra burden of resistance.

The Freedom of Non-Resistance

When you let go of resistance, you free yourself from emotional suffering. You stop battling against the moment and start flowing with it. This doesn't mean you're passive or giving up on trying to improve the situation—it means you accept that the moment is exactly what it is, and from that place of acceptance, you can act with clarity and intention.

Let's go deeper into another example of how resistance compounds suffering:

Real-Life Example of Traffic Jam Resistance:

You're late for an important appointment and you get stuck in a traffic jam. Your initial reaction is to get frustrated, upset, and maybe even angry. You think: *"Why does this always happen to me? I'm going to be late, and this is such a waste of time!"*

In this situation, you're resisting the reality of what is happening. The traffic is happening, and you can't change it. But instead of accepting that it is what it is, you're fighting against it with frustration and judgment. You're telling yourself that the situation should be different, which only makes the situation feel worse.

Now, imagine practicing **non-resistance**. You pause, take a deep breath, and say to yourself:

"This moment is perfect now."

You acknowledge that, yes, being late is frustrating. But instead of adding emotional weight to the situation with anger or judgment, you release it. You might decide to use the extra time to calm yourself, listen to a podcast, or mentally prepare for your appointment. You free yourself from the emotional burden of resistance, which creates space for a clearer, more peaceful mind.

How Non-Resistance Changes the Game

When you stop resisting, you regain your power. You no longer waste energy on trying to change something that you cannot control. Instead, you choose how to engage with the moment. This shift in mindset allows you to act from a place of **calm and clarity**, instead of stress and anxiety.

Real-Life Example of Non-Resistance in Personal Life:

You're facing a disagreement with a close friend. The conversation is difficult, and you feel misunderstood or judged. Your first instinct might be to argue or defend yourself, to make sure your perspective is heard.

But instead of resisting, you take a moment to breathe and **accept** the situation as it is: "This moment is perfect now."

You accept the discomfort and tension. You don't try to control the conversation or force the outcome. You listen more carefully, speak from a place of calm, and find a way to move forward without getting stuck in a cycle of resistance.

Resistance in Action: Turning Stress Into Power

Imagine you're about to give a big presentation. You've prepared for days, but as the moment approaches, your heart starts racing. Your palms sweat. You feel the familiar anxiety creeping up. Maybe your thoughts start spiraling: *"What if I mess up? What if they don't like what I have to say? I should be more confident!"*

Your natural reaction might be to try and suppress those feelings of nervousness. You might attempt to push them down, thinking: *"I shouldn't feel like this. I need to calm down. I need to be perfect."* This is resistance. You're fighting against the moment, wishing it were different.

But with **non-resistance** and the **Perfect Moment Activity**, you have another option. Instead of resisting your anxiety, you pause and say to yourself:

"This moment is perfect now."

You **acknowledge** your nervousness without judgment. Instead of trying to force yourself to feel confident or calm, you accept that the anxiety is part of the moment. It doesn't have to go away for you to perform well. In fact, it's okay to feel nervous. That's part of being human, and it doesn't define your ability to succeed.

By **embracing** the moment as it is, with all the nerves and excitement, you open up a space where you can act **with intention**. You can focus on your breath, calm your mind, and proceed through the experience with a clear head, rather than fighting your emotions. You're not consumed by fear; you're present, engaged, and grounded in the now.

The Freedom of Non-Resistance: A New Way to Engage with Life

The real power of non-resistance comes when you let go of the inner battle. Resistance is a drain on your energy. It's like swimming upstream against a strong current—exhausting and counterproductive. When you stop resisting, you free up that energy to engage more fully with whatever is happening in the moment.

Let's revisit the presentation example. Normally, the anxiety you feel before speaking could turn into a mental battle, distracting you from the task at hand. But by accepting it, you shift your energy from fighting your feelings to acting with purpose. This isn't about eliminating nerves; it's about embracing them, acknowledging that they are part of the moment—and then moving forward despite them. You've freed yourself from the emotional weight that could have held you back.

This freedom of non-resistance can be applied to any situation—whether it's a high-pressure task at work, an uncomfortable conversation, or a tough personal challenge.

More Examples of Non-Resistance in Action
Dealing with a Difficult Conversation:

Imagine you're about to have a difficult conversation with a friend or a colleague. You know there are uncomfortable truths to address, and you feel anxious about how the conversation will unfold. Your first instinct might be to resist the anxiety and suppress the emotions that are surfacing.

Instead of trying to push those feelings away, try the **Perfect Moment Activity**. You stop and say to yourself:

"This moment is perfect now."

You accept that feeling nervous or uncertain is part of this conversation. You're not trying to pretend everything's fine. You're acknowledging the discomfort without judging it. You take a deep breath, focus on the present moment, and approach the conversation with clarity and calm, rather than fear and resistance.

When you accept the situation as it is, you create a space for a productive conversation. You can listen without reacting defensively and speak with intention, without being overwhelmed by emotions or mental distractions.

Facing an Overwhelming Task:

Sometimes we face tasks that feel insurmountable. Maybe it's a huge project at work, an overwhelming to-do list, or an emotionally challenging task. You may look at everything you need to do and feel paralyzed by anxiety or the sheer weight of the responsibility.

Resisting the task by thinking, *"I can't do this"* or *"I'm not ready"* only amplifies the stress. Instead, practice **non-resistance**. Take a moment to breathe, and say to yourself:

"This moment is perfect now."

You recognize that, yes, the task is overwhelming, but it's what you're dealing with right now. You don't need to control the entire outcome. You can focus on what you can do in this moment—taking one step at a time. By accepting the reality of the situation without judgment, you eliminate mental clutter, and instead of resisting, you engage with the task, feeling more clear-headed and empowered.

Embracing an Uncomfortable Situation:

Let's say you're in an uncomfortable social setting. Maybe you're at a party where you don't know many people, or you're in a meeting where you feel out of your depth. It's natural to feel anxious in these situations, but often, the more we resist that discomfort, the more amplified it becomes.

In this case, practicing **non-resistance** would look like this: You acknowledge the unease without trying to push it away. You say to yourself:

"This moment is perfect now."

By embracing the discomfort, you free yourself from unnecessary worry. You don't have to love the situation or feel completely comfortable, but you accept it for what it is. This shift allows you to be present, observe the situation, and engage from a place of calm rather than reactive discomfort.

Next time you feel resistance building up inside you—whether it's anxiety, stress, frustration, or discomfort—remind yourself: **"This moment is perfect now."** Embrace the moment as it is, and let go of the struggle. By accepting life on its terms, you open up a world of freedom, peace, and empowerment.

The Mental Struggle: Living Between Past and Future

We all get caught up in mental distractions. Some people obsess over **the future**, filled with worry and anxiety about things that haven't happened yet:

- *"What if I fail?"*
- *"What if I don't have enough time?"*
- *"What if they don't like me?"*

Other people dwell on **the past**, replaying mistakes, regrets, or missed opportunities:

- *"I should have done this differently."*
- *"Why did I make that mistake?"*
- *"I wish things could go back to the way they were."*

Both mental states keep us trapped in time, and neither gives us access to the full potential of the present moment.

When we're lost in these thought loops, we're missing the richness of now. We're not fully engaged with what's in front of us, and we're not fully alive in the moment. In essence, we're not truly **living**.

The Power of Living in the Present: The Moment is All We Have

The present is where **life happens**. It's where you can **act, make choices**, and **experience reality** as it unfolds. But to experience the present fully, we must let go of our attachments to the past and future.

The **Perfect Moment Activity** is a simple practice that can instantly pull you into the now. Here's how it works:

- **When you catch yourself mentally drifting into the future**—whether with worry, anticipation, or anxiety—simply say to yourself:
  - "This moment is perfect now."
- **When you find yourself lost in the past**, replaying mistakes or wishing for things to be different, stop and say:
  - "This moment is perfect now."

In that simple affirmation, you remind yourself that the present moment is the only one you can truly experience. By repeating **"This moment is perfect now,"** you bring your awareness back to the here and now, stopping the mental drift and centering yourself.

Real-Life Example of Living in the Present

Let's consider a real-life example of the Perfect Moment Activity in action. You're sitting in a meeting, but instead of listening to the discussion, your mind is wandering. You're thinking about the presentation you have to give later, the emails you haven't replied to, or your personal plans for the evening. You're **disconnected** from the present moment.

Now, rather than letting your mind wander further, you stop. You take a deep breath and say to yourself:

"This moment is perfect now."

You shift your attention back to the conversation. Maybe you're not thrilled about the meeting, but it's the reality of the moment. You accept it as it is. Instead of being mentally distracted, you're present, listening, and engaged with what's happening. By grounding yourself in the present, you become more productive and mentally clear. You free yourself from the mental clutter that would otherwise keep you in a state of distraction.

The Benefits of Living in the Present

- **Clarity**: When you focus on the present, your mind becomes clear. You stop getting bogged down by hypothetical scenarios or past mistakes, and you can make decisions based on what's truly happening right now.
- **Less Stress**: When you stop obsessing over the future or the past, you free yourself from unnecessary anxiety. By embracing the present moment, you can feel more relaxed and less overwhelmed.
- **Deeper Connection**: When you're fully present, you engage more deeply with the people and experiences around you. You're not distracted by mental chatter; you're actively participating in life.
- **Increased Peace**: The present moment is the only one you have control over. By focusing on it, you stop resisting reality. This leads to a sense of inner peace, as you accept whatever the moment brings without judgment.
- **Better Decision-Making**: When you're not caught up in the past or future, you can make decisions more effectively. You respond to situations based on the current circumstances, instead of being driven by past regrets or future fears.

When to Use the Perfect Moment Activity

The **Perfect Moment Activity** is not just for "big moments" like giving a presentation or attending a high-stakes meeting. It can be applied to any moment of your day:

- **During a stressful commute**: Instead of getting frustrated with traffic or delays, say to yourself, **"This moment is perfect now."** Accept that the traffic is what it is and choose to focus on your breath or use the time to mentally prepare for the day.
- **In a difficult conversation**: When you feel the urge to react emotionally to what someone is saying, pause and say, **"This moment is perfect now."** You accept the conversation as it is and choose to engage from a place of calm and clarity.
- **When you're feeling overwhelmed**: When your to-do list feels endless and your mind is racing with all the things you have to do,

stop and say, **"This moment is perfect now."** You ground yourself in the present, acknowledge that you can only do one thing at a time, and focus on the next step.

- **In everyday interactions**: Whether you're talking with a friend, eating a meal, or enjoying a quiet moment, remind yourself: **"This moment is perfect now."** By embracing the present, you deepen your connection with life and with others.

Example: Navigating Personal Disappointment

Let's take another example: You've just received disappointing news about a personal goal you've been working towards. Maybe you didn't get the promotion you were hoping for, or a personal project didn't turn out the way you imagined. Naturally, this news triggers disappointment, maybe even some self-doubt.

Rather than allowing that feeling of disappointment to dictate your entire emotional state, you apply the **Perfect Moment Activity**. You stop, take a deep breath, and say to yourself, **"This moment is perfect now."**

You acknowledge the disappointment without judgment. You recognize that the disappointment is a part of your emotional spectrum, but it does not define you. By accepting the present moment—disappointment and all—you give yourself permission to experience the feeling fully, while maintaining your emotional equilibrium.

This allows you to process the disappointment without spiraling into negativity or self-criticism. Instead of getting lost in regret or self-doubt, you regain your balance, take stock of the lesson, and move forward with clarity.

As you continue to practice the **Perfect Moment Activity**, you'll notice that emotional resilience becomes a natural part of your mindset. You will find yourself more equipped to handle whatever challenges or setbacks arise, with a sense of **calm** and **acceptance** that allows you to remain grounded and focused.

The more you practice, the more your emotional resilience will grow—until it becomes an **unshakable foundation** for facing life's inevitable ups and downs.

This may appear repetitive, but I MUST tattoo the concept into your mind:

Here are **8 common "Perfect Moment" scenarios** where you can apply the "This moment is perfect now" mindset:

Traffic Jam or Delay

- **Scenario:** You're stuck in heavy traffic or waiting for a delayed flight, and frustration starts building.
- **Perfect Moment Mindset:** "This moment is perfect now."
- **What to Do:** Instead of focusing on the time lost or the stress, embrace the moment. Use it as an opportunity to relax, reflect, or simply practice deep breathing.

An Unexpected Setback at Work or School

- **Scenario:** A project gets delayed, you make a mistake, or you miss a deadline. There's a sense of failure or frustration.
- **Perfect Moment Mindset:** "This moment is perfect now."
- **What to Do:** Instead of beating yourself up, recognize that setbacks are a natural part of growth. Acknowledge that this is a chance to learn, correct course, or adjust expectations.

An Argument or Conflict

- **Scenario:** You find yourself in a disagreement with a friend, family member, or colleague.
- **Perfect Moment Mindset:** "This moment is perfect now."
- **What to Do:** Rather than escalating the conflict, pause and acknowledge that this moment is an opportunity to learn about the other person, practice patience, and find common ground.

Financial Stress or Worry

- **Scenario:** You're experiencing financial pressure, whether it's unexpected expenses, not having enough savings, or debt.
- **Perfect Moment Mindset:** "This moment is perfect now."

- **What to Do:** Instead of spiraling into panic, breathe and recognize that stress and worry don't solve problems. This moment is an opportunity to reassess your priorities, make a new plan, or simply be mindful of what you already have.

Physical Discomfort or Illness

- **Scenario:** You're not feeling well, whether it's a minor headache, a cold, or something more significant.
- **Perfect Moment Mindset:** "This moment is perfect now."
- **What to Do:** Rather than resisting the discomfort, allow yourself to rest and be present with your body. Use this moment to practice self-care, appreciate the wisdom of your body, and focus on healing.

Feeling Overwhelmed by Responsibilities

- **Scenario:** You feel overwhelmed by the sheer amount of tasks and responsibilities—whether it's work, family obligations, or personal goals.
- **Perfect Moment Mindset:** "This moment is perfect now."
- **What to Do:** Rather than getting caught up in the chaos, take a deep breath and recognize that this is the perfect time to reset priorities, ask for help, or take a short break to clear your mind.

Negative Self-Talk or Low Self-Esteem

- **Scenario:** You catch yourself thinking "I'm not good enough," "I can't do this," or "I always mess up."
- **Perfect Moment Mindset:** "This moment is perfect now."
- **What to Do:** Instead of allowing these thoughts to spiral, acknowledge them as part of the human experience and let them go. Focus on your strengths, reframe your thinking, and remind yourself that you are always capable of growth.

The Mundane or Routine Moments

- **Scenario:** You're doing something mundane—washing the dishes, standing in line, or waiting for a meeting to start.
- **Perfect Moment Mindset:** "This moment is perfect now."
- **What to Do:** Instead of feeling impatient or wishing for the task to be over, choose to be fully present. Notice the sensations, sounds, and feelings in the moment. This small practice of mindfulness can help you experience peace even in the most routine moments.

Practicing the Perfect Moment Activity teaches you to accept each moment as it comes, reduce emotional resistance, and respond with intention, building resilience, peace, and clarity in the process.

Activity 3: How to Grow Your Charisma

Charisma Activity

What is Charisma?

Charisma isn't something you're born with. It's not some elusive trait that a lucky few are gifted. Charisma is energy—raw, powerful energy—that you project outward. It's the presence you carry, the force that draws people to you, makes them listen, and makes them want to be around you.

Think of it like this: when a charismatic person walks into a room, everyone knows it. They don't have to say a word. It's their energy that fills the space. It's in the way they move, the way they speak, the way they make others feel. Charisma is more than just physical attraction or charm—it's the power that flows from within.

It's the energy of leadership when you step up and take charge. It's the calm, clear focus that draws people in and makes them want to follow your lead. It's the kindness that makes others feel safe, heard, and valued.

Charismatic people are magnetic because they radiate something you can't always put into words. It's the feeling that you want to be near them, to work with them, to listen to them, or to be inspired by them. They carry that invisible, almost tangible energy that others can feel even if they can't explain why.

In short, charisma isn't a trait you're stuck with—it's an energy you can cultivate and unleash. And once you learn how to harness it, you'll see how it can transform not just how others perceive you, but how you move through the world.

What is missing in your life? What kind of energy do you need right now? Love? Confidence? Compassion? Leadership? Focus? Vision? Whatever it is, the Charisma Activity's got your back. You want to walk into a room and own it? You want people to feel you the second you step up? This is the tool that'll give you that. You don't need to wait for it to come naturally. You don't need to hope it just happens. You can *create* it.

Love? You're going to feel it. Confidence? You're going to radiate it. Compassion? You'll be the one people turn to. Leadership? You'll lead without hesitation. Focus? It's going to laser in. Vision? You'll see the path clearly and act on it.

You think you need all this from the outside world? Forget it. The Charisma Activity puts the power in your hands. You bring it out, you use it, and you make it happen. It's time to level up. Let's do this.

If you want to stay sharp, stay energized, and dominate in any situation, you've got to work on your charisma. It's not some fluffy feel-good concept, it's a weapon. A weapon that gives you authority, makes people pay attention, and gets things done. You want to crush it under pressure? You want to show up when it matters? Then you need to control your energy, and you need to control it fast.

The Charisma Activity? It's not a game. It's a drill to tap into that inner power you're sitting on. That's right, you've got a personal energy reservoir. Time to stop sitting on it. Your presence, your influence, your leadership – they're all tied to how much energy you've got and how you use it.

Don't show up flat. Don't show up tired. Get your energy in check, boost your authority, and make your mark wherever you go. This isn't just for the easy days. This is about showing up, every time, no matter what the challenge is. You get it? Good. Now get to work.

Let's begin with love.

Step 1: Cultivate the Feeling of Love

Here's the deal – you want to own the room, you want to be magnetic? Start with this. First thing every morning, before your feet hit the floor, you've got two minutes. That's it. Two minutes to flood your body with the feeling of love.

Think back to a moment that made you feel on top of the world. Maybe it was when you found someone you'd die for, or when you did something that had you feeling like a king. It could've been a life-changing trip or just that day you felt unstoppable. Whatever it is, bring that feeling to the front of your mind. *Feel it.* Don't just think about it. Bring it into your chest, into your heart, and let it expand.

Love. It's the fuel that'll fire you up. It's that warm, powerful feeling that opens you up and makes people take notice. Let it fill your body, let it power you. If you can bring this feeling to your core every day, you're going to start carrying that energy everywhere you go. You get this right, and you'll be magnetic. Now, get to work.

Step 2: Bring the Energy to Your Third Eye

Now that you've got that love flowing through you, it's time to focus. You've got the energy, but we're not just letting it wander around. You're going to guide it. Bring that power to your third eye – that spot right between your eyebrows, just above the bridge of your nose.

You don't need to feel it at first. Doesn't matter if you can't physically sense it. Visualize it. That's right – *see* it there. The mind is a powerful tool. If you train it right, visualization works just as well as any physical sensation. Focus that energy, lock it in. Keep that feeling of love alive as you direct it to your third eye.

This isn't some woo-woo nonsense. This is focus. This is control. This is you mastering your energy. Do it daily, and it'll become second nature. Now, make it happen.

Step 3: Extend the Energy to Your Eyes

Alright, you've got the love locked in and your third eye dialed in. Now, we're taking it up a notch. From that spot between your eyebrows, let that energy flow into your eyes. Let it seep into your eyelids and spread across your eyes. You might not feel it right away – doesn't matter. Visualize it. Picture that warm, expansive energy filling your eyes, making them bright, clear, and full of life.

This isn't about just feeling good, this is about sending a message to your body and mind that you are operating at a whole new level. Eyes are the window to the soul. When you fill them with positive energy, you signal strength, presence, and openness. Assume it's happening, even if the feeling is faint. The more you do this, the stronger it gets. You're building belief in the power of your energy. Get it done.

Step 4: Radiate Love to Others

You've got the energy, you've got the focus, now it's time to *give* it. You're not here just to fill yourself up; you're here to spread that power. Start with 2-3 people you care about deeply – people who have your back, people who make you feel safe, supported, and loved. Could be family, friends, pets, or even a place that brings you peace. Focus on them.

Now, let that energy move from your eyes, like a beam of light, and channel it straight to them. Don't just think it—*feel it*. As you do, whisper to yourself: "I love you." Send them that energy, send them that power. Don't hold back.

Now, don't stop there. Take it a step further. Send that same energy to 2-3 people you don't exactly vibe with. People you don't have warm feelings toward. This isn't about them, it's about you. You're raising your energy, not theirs. Send that beam of love their way. As you do, whisper: "I love you."

This is about breaking through your limits. You want to level up? Start with love, and let it expand outward. Keep doing this, and you'll find yourself standing taller, stronger, and more connected. Time to push past the comfort zone. Let it fly.

Step 5: Send Love to Yourself

Alright, now it's time to turn that love inward. You've given it to others, now give it to the most important person in the room – *you*. From your third eye, let that powerful energy flow down through your body, filling every inch of you. Let it wash over you, flooding your chest, your core, your arms, your legs. Let it consume you.

Once you're fully saturated with that loving energy, say it – and mean it: "I love you." You've just reinforced the foundation of your charisma. This isn't about ego, it's about recognizing your own power, your own worth. You can't give what you don't have.

And this is just the beginning. Love is the base. But don't stop here. With practice, you'll learn to channel other energies—confidence, focus, vision, authority—and bring them into your charisma. But for now, this love energy is your rock. Build on it. Strengthen it. Make it unshakable. This is how you become magnetic. Now, lock it in.

Step 6: Sharpen Your Charismatic Energy

Once you've locked in the basic love energy and made it your foundation, it's time to take it to the next level. Charisma isn't just about one type of energy—it's about tailoring and sharpening that energy to amplify specific qualities you want to project. You want people to be drawn to your intelligence? Your leadership? Your confidence? It's time to specialize.

Start with intelligence. If you want others to see you as insightful, sharp, and full of ideas, focus on those moments when you've been at your best. Recall the times you were sharp, innovative, or had that sudden spark of genius. Get that feeling in your body. Visualize it.

Instead of focusing on love, shift your attention to *intelligence*. Picture it filling your heart, your chest, your core. Let that energy radiate outward, just like you did with love. Move that energy from your third eye to your eyes, and then direct it toward others with the same process as before.

Do this same exercise for other attributes you want to amplify—whether that's leadership, vision, confidence, or anything else that plays a crucial role in your charisma. Want to command respect in a room? Focus on leadership. Want people to feel your vision and follow your direction? Dial up your sense of clarity and foresight.

The more you practice sharpening each of these energies, the stronger and more magnetic you'll become. The key is consistency. The more you hone in on specific qualities, the more powerful they'll be when you need them. This is how you build a charisma that's not just wide-reaching, but laser-focused and unstoppable. Get it done.

Step 7: Beyond the Morning Ritual

Listen up, because this is where the rubber hits the road. The morning ritual? That's just your warm-up. It's the foundation. It sets the tone. But if you're serious about mastering this, you don't stop there. You take that same energy, that same presence, and you carry it with you throughout the day. Everywhere you go, you take that power with you, and you use it.

Now, let's break this down:

- **At the Office:**
  When you walk into that office, don't just shuffle in like you're on autopilot. You're not some drone going through the motions. You *own* that space. Before you even step into that room, you flood it with your energy. Imagine love — I know, it sounds corny, but stick with me — imagine it as a force, like a light pouring out of you. You're not walking in empty-handed; you're carrying an invisible force field with you. You don't need to announce it. Just walk in, and let that feeling

radiate. And if you've got the guts, whisper to yourself, "I love you," as a reminder. But don't just say it. *Feel it.* It's contagious, and it will hit everyone around you.

- **In Meetings or Social Situations:**
  You've got a meeting, a dinner, a networking event? This isn't just about "getting through it." This is about dominating it. You walk in, and you look everyone in the eye and mentally *fall in love* with them. Not in some creepy, romantic way — you're not here to swoon. But you do have to tap into something deeper, something genuine. You *connect* with people before you even speak. Imagine your energy reaching them, like an invisible thread pulling you together. Do this, and watch how quickly people start leaning in, trusting you, and hanging on every word. It's not magic. It's presence. And you've got it in spades.

- **In Public Places:**
  This one's simple: everywhere you go, you're an ambassador of energy. The coffee shop? Send out waves of love. The grocery store? Same thing. On the bus or subway? You better believe it. It's about being aware of the world around you. It's about engaging with it, not just moving through it. The second you start sending out that love energy — not as some grand gesture, but as a constant hum in the background — people notice. They can feel it. That magnetic, unspoken connection. They'll start responding to you differently. Trust me. This isn't about making them notice you for the wrong reasons; it's about establishing a presence that demands attention.

This isn't some feel-good exercise. This is strategy. The more you practice this, the more you'll start seeing it work in every interaction. You won't just be another guy in the room. You'll be the guy people *gravitate toward*. You'll be magnetic. The energy you send out will change the whole dynamic of the room — and when that happens, you're in control. You're the one shaping the conversation. You're the one leading the charge. You just have to commit to doing it, every single day, without fail.

You ready for that? Then don't waste time. Get after it.

Step 8: Use the Energy You Need

Alright, pay attention. This step is all about *control* — control over your energy, your presence, your impact. Charisma isn't just about showing up and hoping for the best. It's about being deliberate. It's about knowing *exactly* what energy you need in a given moment, and then *channeling* that energy like a force of nature.

Here's how you do it:

- **Want to Command Attention?**

  If you're walking into a room and you need people to *sit up straight* and listen, then it's time to turn on the leadership energy. This is the energy that makes people stop what they're doing and pay attention. It's the energy of decisiveness, authority, and unwavering confidence. You don't have to yell to make your presence felt. No, it's much more subtle. You tap into this energy, and you project it. You stand taller. You move with purpose. Your voice is calm, but firm. When you speak, people lean in. This isn't a *show* — this is you owning the room with your presence. You're not asking for respect, you're demanding it.

- **Need to Build Cooperation and Connection?**

  When you need to draw people in, get them to trust you, to feel like they're *with* you, that's when you tap into love energy. This is the energy of kindness, empathy, and shared purpose. You're not here to dominate; you're here to unify. It's the energy that makes people feel understood, respected, and valued. You use it to disarm resistance, to create an environment where people feel safe to share their thoughts, their ideas, their vulnerabilities. This isn't about being soft. It's about being *strong* in your ability to connect. It's about creating a space where people want to work with you, not against you.

- **Want to Be Seen as a Visionary?**

  When you need people to see you as someone who's ahead of the curve, someone with *big ideas*, you need to amplify the visionary energy. This is the energy of creativity, inspiration, and bold thinking. You tap into the energy of the future, the energy of possibility. You communicate with conviction and passion, not just about what is, but about what could be. This energy makes people follow you not because they have to, but because they *want to* — they see your vision and they want to be a part of it.

But here's the kicker: *You're not stuck with just one energy.* You don't have to be locked into one mode, hoping you're in the right frame of mind. The beauty of this is that you can shift and adapt. If you need to be authoritative in one moment and empathetic the next, you can do it. You just have to *learn* how to switch gears on command. It takes practice, but you've got the tools.

This isn't about pretending to be something you're not. It's about being *who you are* at the core, but with the precision to harness whatever energy is going to get the job done. Every situation calls for a different approach. You've got the ability to step into any role — leader, collaborator, visionary — and project the exact energy you need to crush it.

So, let's be clear. You don't need to "try" to be charismatic. You just need to *choose* the energy that fits the situation, and project it with total confidence. And if you retrain your mind to focus on these powerful, positive energies, you'll find yourself *operating on a level* most people can't even comprehend.

Now get out there and use it.

Charisma: It's Not Inherited, It's Developed

Let me make one thing clear: charisma isn't something that magically falls into your lap because you were born with a "charming" gene. Forget that nonsense. Charisma is a *skill*, not a trait. You can *develop* it, you can *sharpen* it, and you can make it your own. Just like any skill — whether it's playing the piano, hitting a baseball, or lifting weights — charisma comes down to practice and repetition. It's about managing your energy, understanding how to project it, and learning when to dial it up or tone it down.

So here's the deal. If you want to develop real, lasting charisma, you have to commit to showing up every day and practicing the right way. You need to put in the work to direct your energy with precision. No one's going to hand you this on a silver platter, but if you've got the grit to keep working at it — and the mental clarity to understand how energy works — then charisma will become second nature. And that's when things change. You won't just walk into a room — you'll *command* it.

Now, let's talk about energy. Charisma is about *projecting energy*. The *Charisma Activity* is your playbook for how to manage, amplify, and direct your energy. It's not some abstract feel-good concept. It's about taking control of your presence, raising the vibration around you, and pulling people in without even saying a word. You do that, and people will start reacting to you differently. They'll feel the pull of your energy, the strength of your presence — they won't be able to ignore it.

So, you start with **love energy**. Why? Because that's where it all begins. It's the foundation. If you don't have a solid base of love — genuine care for others, for the world around you — none of the other energies will land right. If you can learn to channel love into everything you do, it will shape how you connect with others, how you influence them, and how you lead.

But love energy isn't some weak, fluffy, "be nice to everyone" stuff. This is a force. It's the power to unite, to create trust, and to make people feel seen and heard. When you start practicing it, you'll see how much it shifts the room. People will start responding to you differently. You'll be magnetic, drawing people toward you with just your presence. It doesn't happen overnight, but keep at it — every day, with intent — and soon you'll be living it.

Consistency is key. You don't have to be perfect. But you do have to show up every day with intention, with energy, and with focus. Do that, and your charisma will go from a flicker to a flame — and people won't be able to ignore the heat you're radiating.

Six Common Types of Energy for Charisma

Now let's get tactical. The Charisma Activity isn't about just one energy. It's about *mastering* multiple kinds of energy and knowing how to dial in the right one at the right time. Charisma is situational. It's about projecting the exact energy you need to get the result you want — whether it's building rapport, commanding respect, inspiring a team, or creating excitement. So here are six types of energy you can tap into, and examples of how to use each one.

Love Energy

This is the cornerstone. Love energy is about connection. It's about fostering cooperation and building relationships. This is the energy that makes people feel comfortable, understood, and valued. It's about putting the other person first, understanding their needs, and creating an environment where they feel safe.

- **How to use it:** Let's say you're walking into a meeting with a team that's been stressed out or underperforming. You don't need to come in like a drill sergeant or a hardass. Instead, take a moment before you enter. Set an intention to connect with the people in the room. Mentally, send out a wave of love — not the romantic kind, but a sense of empathy and goodwill. As you walk in, make eye contact, nod, and let that energy radiate from you. During the meeting, really listen. Show that you care about what's being said. When people feel that, they'll follow you.

Leadership Energy

This is your "command the room" energy. When you need to step up, stand tall, and be the one people look to for direction, leadership energy is what you need. This energy is about authority without being overbearing. It's about presence — when you walk in, the room feels your confidence. People start to pay attention.

- **How to use it:** Picture yourself walking into a big meeting, or presenting to a group of people. When you enter, stand tall, chin up. No slouching, no hesitating. Walk as if the space belongs to you. Speak with clarity and authority. Use pauses to create weight, not to fill silence. When people are unsure, they'll look to you for answers, and you'll give them confidently.

Visionary Energy

Visionary energy is what makes people want to follow you. It's the energy of innovation, bold ideas, and seeing possibilities that others can't. If you want to be a true leader — someone who inspires people to move toward a big, bold future — you need to channel visionary energy.

- **How to use it:** Imagine you're presenting a new idea to your team, or pitching something big to investors. Don't just talk about facts or numbers. Paint a picture. Get people excited about the future, not just the present. Use language that connects the dots between what's possible and what can be. Talk about vision, not just what's in front of you right now. People follow visionaries because they want to be part of something bigger.

Confidence Energy

Without confidence, none of this matters. Confidence is the backbone of charisma. When you exude confidence, people believe in you before you even say a word. Confidence energy is quiet, unshakable belief in your own abilities. It's not cocky, it's assured.

- **How to use it:** The next time you're presenting or even in a casual conversation, take your time. Don't rush. Speak clearly, with authority. Own the room. Look people in the eye. Move with purpose. People may not remember every word you say, but they'll remember the energy you put off — and confidence is magnetic.

Playful Energy

Sometimes, you need to lighten the mood, break tension, and show people you can be approachable. Playful energy is all about disarming people, making them laugh, and creating an atmosphere of fun. It's about balance — knowing when to be serious and when to make people feel comfortable by being lighthearted.

- **How to use it:** In a tense meeting or a stressful situation, crack a joke. Not a stand-up comedy routine, just something light that gets people to laugh. Use humor to break the ice, and show people you don't take yourself too seriously. A little self-deprecating humor can go a long way to building rapport and making people want to be around you.

Mystery Energy

People are drawn to mystery. When you have mystery energy, people are intrigued by you, curious, and they want to know more. This energy is about creating an aura of unpredictability. It keeps people on their toes, constantly wanting to figure you out.

- **How to use it:** Don't give away everything right away. Be selective with your words. When you speak, don't over-explain — leave some things unsaid. Use pauses, allow the silence to work for you. Keep some of your cards close to the chest, and let people wonder what's next. When you do this, people are drawn to you because they want to figure you out.

Now Here's The Key

You don't need to master all six energies at once. Start with one. Focus on it. Build it. Don't try to juggle all the types from day one. Once you've got one down, add another. The more you practice, the more you'll begin to naturally shift between energies depending on the situation. You'll be able to amplify whatever energy you need at the moment.

If you commit to this process — showing up every day, practicing, refining — you'll transform. You won't just be charismatic; you'll be *unstoppable*. And in the end, that's what charisma is: the ability to command a room, to connect with people on a deeper level, and to lead with unshakeable confidence. It's work, but it's worth it. Now get out there and start cultivating it.

Compassion Energy: The Power of Connection

Let me be clear: compassion is not weakness. It's one of the most powerful forces you can wield, and it's something you can develop with intention and practice. Compassion energy is an unspoken connection you create with people that makes them feel seen, understood, and valued. It's the ability to meet someone where they are — without judgment, without conditions — and let them know that they're not alone. In a world that often feels disconnected and cold, compassion is the bridge that brings people together.

Compassion is about more than just feeling bad for someone; it's about deeply *understanding* their pain, their struggle, or their challenge, and offering genuine support. It's the foundation of trust, and it creates rapport like nothing else. When you practice compassion energy, you don't just empathize with others; you become a source of comfort and reassurance. People are drawn to that energy because it's real. They feel your sincerity, and they want to be around you.

So, how do you tap into this energy and project it in a way that makes a difference? Here's how to apply compassion energy in your day-to-day interactions, and how to make it an essential part of your charismatic presence.

How to Apply Compassion Energy

Compassion isn't something you can force; it's an energy you *cultivate* and then share with others. It starts inside, and once you feel it, you can project it outward. The following steps will help you access that energy and make it part of who you are.

Step 1: Recall a Moment of Compassion

Think about a time when you showed compassion to someone or when you received it yourself. Maybe it was a time when a friend opened up to you and you just listened without judgment, or a moment when someone extended a hand to help you through a difficult time. Feel that warmth in your chest. That's the energy we're after.

Compassion is rooted in shared experience. When you tap into it, you're connecting to something real. It could be a memory of comforting a friend in crisis, or it could be a moment of someone showing you care during a tough period. Don't rush through this step. You need to *feel* that warmth — that sense of human connection. Once you feel that spark, you're ready to move forward.

Step 2: Bring That Energy to Your Mind

Now, take that warm, compassionate energy and focus on bringing it to your third eye — the space between your eyebrows, just above your nose. This is where your intuition and awareness are centered. As you bring the compassion energy here, visualize it filling your mind with kindness, understanding, and clarity. Let it settle in. Allow your thoughts to soften, like a fog of warmth, clearing away any judgments or impatience.

When you do this, you're creating the mental framework to connect with others in an open, non-judgmental way. It's not just about feeling sorry for someone; it's about understanding them deeply and meeting them where they are. This is how you project compassion — you create space in your mind to offer care without conditions.

Step 3: Move the Compassion Into Your Eyes

Compassion is felt through your eyes. Your gaze speaks volumes. When you're communicating with someone, whether it's in a tough conversation or a casual exchange, the warmth of your compassion should be reflected in your eyes. You can't fake this. Compassionate energy softens your gaze and makes your eyes more inviting, more understanding. This step is about **showing** your compassion without words.

Take a deep breath, and let the energy you've gathered in your mind flow down into your eyes. Picture the beam of compassion radiating from your eyes, offering understanding and care. Imagine that when you look at someone, they feel seen — not just physically, but emotionally and psychologically. They know you're there for them. The key here is to be fully present. No distractions. No rushing. Just genuine presence and care.

Step 4: Project Compassion to Those Around You

Once you've activated the compassion energy inside you, it's time to send it out. Visualize the compassion extending from you, enveloping others in a comforting embrace. Imagine the people you're interacting with being bathed in that compassionate energy, feeling heard, understood, and supported. Whether it's a one-on-one conversation or a group setting, let that energy flow through you and into the space.

Think of this like an invisible light that you shine on others. In a group setting, for example, if you're facilitating a discussion where emotions are running high, imagine that light extending to everyone involved, helping to calm the tension. Let them feel safe, open, and free to express themselves. When people feel comfortable and supported, they're more likely to open up and collaborate with you.

Step 5: Affirm Compassion with a Quiet Declaration

As you continue to radiate compassion, whisper to yourself: "I am compassionate." This is a simple but powerful affirmation. It helps ground you and reinforces your intention. It reminds you that compassion isn't something you *do* — it's something you *are*. The more you affirm this, the more naturally it will flow from you. You'll start to embody compassion in every interaction, and that energy will become a cornerstone of your presence.

You don't need to say the words out loud. Just say it in your mind, and feel the wave of kindness extend from you to everyone around you. This isn't just about comforting people in difficult moments; it's about building a reputation for being someone who always has a genuine interest in others, who listens without judgment, and who offers support when needed.

When to Use Compassion Energy

So, when is the right time to tap into compassion energy? There are plenty of scenarios where this energy can make a massive difference in how people respond to you. Here are a few key situations where compassion energy is indispensable:

Emotionally Charged Situations

When emotions are high — whether in a conflict, a difficult conversation, or a tense meeting — compassion energy is your go-to. If you're dealing with someone who is upset, angry, or frustrated, the last thing they need is a cold, detached response. Instead, they need to feel understood. Compassion helps defuse tense situations by showing that you care and that you're there to support them, not challenge them.

Example: Imagine a situation where a colleague is visibly upset during a meeting because their project has been rejected. They're defensive, and their emotions are running high. Rather than countering with logic or pushing for your own ideas, you tap into compassion. You listen to their concerns without judgment, nodding to show you're paying attention, and your eyes soften to convey your understanding. You may not have an immediate solution, but by acknowledging their feelings, you create an opening for dialogue. This makes the other person feel seen, and often, that's enough to bring the tension down.

Customer Service, Healthcare, or Empathy-Driven Jobs

In roles like customer service or healthcare, compassion is essential. Whether you're helping an upset customer, listening to a patient's concerns, or working with a client who's going through a rough time, your ability to project compassion can make all the difference in how they feel about the interaction.

Example: Think about a healthcare worker responding to a worried parent in the ER. The parent is anxious about their child's condition, and emotions are high. A healthcare worker who taps into compassion, listens attentively, and speaks with gentle understanding can make all the difference. Instead of just offering technical information, they make the parent feel heard, valued, and supported.

Creating Safe, Open Atmospheres in Group Settings

In group settings, whether it's a meeting, a team-building event, or a social gathering, compassion helps create a safe space for people to express themselves without fear of judgment. It helps bring down the walls people put up and encourages honest, open communication.

Example: During a brainstorming session, some people may hesitate to share their ideas because they're unsure if they'll be shot down. As the leader, you can use compassion energy to create an environment where people feel safe to express their thoughts. When you listen with genuine interest, make eye contact, and respond with understanding, it encourages others to do the same.

Compassion energy is one of the most powerful forces you can tap into. It creates connection, builds trust, and fosters an atmosphere of support and understanding. Whether you're navigating emotionally charged situations, offering help in customer service, or simply leading with empathy, compassion will elevate your charisma and leave a lasting impact on those around you. Make it a practice to tap into this energy every day, and watch how it transforms your relationships and interactions.

Leadership Energy: Commanding Presence and Direction

If you want to lead people, you need more than just a title or a position of power. You need to embody leadership. Leadership energy isn't just about giving orders; it's about inspiring confidence, creating a sense of purpose, and motivating people to follow you. It's about projecting authority and vision in a way that others can't ignore. Whether you're leading a team, managing a project, or guiding a group, leadership energy is what draws people to you and makes them want to follow your example. It's the difference between being a manager and being a *leader*.

Leadership isn't about domination; it's about direction. You are the force that moves others forward. People follow leaders because they see something in them that inspires action. They trust the leader's vision, and they want to be part of that vision. Leadership energy is about creating that trust, projecting confidence, and guiding people toward a goal.

Here's how you can harness and project leadership energy. Follow these steps, and you'll begin to step into your role as a true leader, no matter the situation.

How to Apply Leadership Energy

Leadership energy isn't something that can be faked; it must be embodied from within. It's an internal energy that, once you tap into it, radiates outward and commands attention. It's not about being the loudest in the room — it's about being the most *present*, the most *confident*, and the most *purposeful*. Here's how you can begin to activate that leadership energy:

Step 1: Recall a Leadership Moment

Think back to a time when you were in a leadership role, whether formal or informal, and people were drawn to your guidance. Maybe it was a time when you successfully led a team on a project, or perhaps it was a moment when you stepped up in a crisis and everyone followed your lead. Recall the strength you felt in that moment — the confidence, the clarity, and the sense of direction you exuded.

When you remember a time when your leadership energy was at its peak, you tap into the power of that experience. Leadership energy is built on your past successes, and by recalling those moments, you reawaken that sense of authority and influence within yourself.

Step 2: Visualize the Energy Moving from Your Heart to Your Third Eye

Now, take the energy you've recalled from your leadership moment and bring it to your heart. The heart is where your personal strength resides — your courage, your resolve, and your inner fire. From there, visualize that energy moving upward to your third eye, the space between your eyebrows. This is your center of vision and clarity. It's where you're able to see the bigger picture and make decisions that align with your purpose.

As the energy moves upward, imagine it filling you with a sense of direction and purpose. It's not just a vague idea; it's a sharp, focused vision of where you're going and how you're going to get there. This is the energy of a leader who doesn't just *have* a goal — they know exactly how to achieve it. They have clarity of vision, and they inspire confidence in others to follow them.

Step 3: Radiate Leadership Energy Through Your Eyes

Leadership energy doesn't need to be shouted from the rooftops. It's not about being brash or demanding attention. The most powerful leaders have a commanding presence that is felt without a word being spoken. The eyes are the window to the soul, and they are also the window to your leadership energy.

With your leadership energy moving through your third eye, imagine it radiating outward through your eyes. When you speak, your eyes should be steady, direct, and full of purpose. When you make eye contact, people should feel your confidence, your vision, and your strength. Your gaze should carry a message: "I know where we're going, and I'm taking you with me."

Leadership energy in the eyes is about *being present* and *projecting certainty*. When you speak, your eyes should reinforce your words. They should signal clarity and conviction. When you walk into a room or lead a meeting, your eyes should tell people that you're in charge — but not in an authoritarian way. It's the kind of presence that draws people to you, makes them want to follow your lead, and gives them the assurance that they are in good hands.

Step 4: Send Leadership Energy to Those You Lead

Leadership isn't just about projecting strength — it's about *connecting* with the people you lead. Once you've tapped into your leadership energy, it's time to send that energy to the people who are under your guidance, whether that's a team at work, a group of friends, or a family member.

Think of leadership as a transmission of energy. Once you've cultivated your own leadership energy, you need to project it outward, directing it toward those you lead. Imagine that energy moving from you into the people you're interacting with. Picture them receiving that energy and feeling inspired, motivated, and reassured.

Whether you're leading a meeting, a project, or a group, when you project leadership energy, the people around you feel it. They will follow your example, adopt your sense of purpose, and work together to achieve the vision you've set. The best leaders don't just command — they inspire.

Step 5: Whisper to Yourself: "I Am a Leader"

Leadership energy needs to be reinforced internally. While it's essential to project it outwardly, you also need to affirm it within yourself. Whisper to yourself: "I am a leader." This affirmation is crucial. It helps ground your energy and solidify your identity as a leader. Leadership isn't something you do — it's something you *are*. When you repeat this affirmation, you rewire your mindset and internalize that leadership is part of your core identity.

By affirming "I am a leader," you remind yourself that you don't need permission to lead — you already have what it takes. You are in charge of your own success, and you are capable of leading others to victory.

When to Use Leadership Energy

Leadership energy should be harnessed when you need to step up and take charge of a situation. It's not just for formal leadership roles — anyone can benefit from developing this energy. Here are some scenarios when leadership energy is essential:

Leading Meetings, Teams, or Projects

Whenever you're in a position to lead a group, whether in a meeting or on a project, leadership energy is your most valuable tool. People will look to you for direction. If you project confidence and clarity, they will follow your lead. You don't need to be the loudest or the most outspoken person in the room, but you do need to be the one who inspires confidence.

Example: In a project meeting where a team is feeling uncertain about how to move forward, your leadership energy can guide them. You walk in, project calm confidence, make eye contact, and speak with clarity. Your words offer a clear path forward, and people naturally gravitate toward your vision. They feel reassured and motivated, and as a result, the team works together more cohesively.

Moments That Require Inspiration or Motivation

There will be times when people around you — whether your team, your friends, or your family — are discouraged, unmotivated, or unsure of the path ahead. That's when leadership energy becomes indispensable. As a leader, it's your job to inspire, to ignite that spark of enthusiasm and confidence in others.

Example: Imagine you're working with a team that's been through several failed attempts at a goal. They're tired, frustrated, and losing hope. It's your job to reignite their energy and confidence. By projecting leadership energy, you remind them of the bigger picture, of the purpose behind the project, and of their ability to succeed. Your energy becomes a beacon, drawing them back into action.

Taking Charge of Situations and Providing Clear Direction

There will be times when situations are chaotic, or people are unsure of what to do. In those moments, leadership energy is about taking charge. You provide the clarity, the direction, and the confidence needed to move forward. People follow leaders because they trust that the leader knows where they are going.

Example: During a crisis at work or in your personal life, the ability to project leadership energy can make all the difference. When everyone else is scrambling, you stand firm, offering clear, decisive actions. Your leadership energy reassures people and gives them a roadmap for how to proceed.

Leadership energy is one of the most essential tools you can cultivate. It's about inspiring others, offering direction, and guiding people toward a shared vision. By following the steps to activate and project your leadership energy, you'll find that you become not just a leader in name but a true source of influence and inspiration. Leadership energy is what makes people want to follow you, and it's what drives teams and projects toward success. Don't wait for permission to lead — start embodying leadership energy today, and watch how it transforms your interactions and your impact on the world.

Focused Energy: Mastering Concentration and Presence

Focused energy is a critical component of charisma and leadership. It's the ability to zone in on a task, eliminate distractions, and give your full attention to what matters most in the present moment. In a world overflowing with distractions — from notifications to multitasking demands — the ability to focus is more valuable than ever. When you master focused energy, you gain control over your time, your tasks, and your mental space. Whether you're working on a complex project, solving a problem, or creating something new, the ability to focus will set you apart and elevate your effectiveness.

But focus isn't something that just happens; it's a skill you can cultivate, refine, and amplify. Focused energy is about harnessing your attention and keeping it on the task at hand until completion, rather than letting your mind wander or being pulled in a hundred different directions. It's about the laser-like precision that comes from concentration, discipline, and the ability to shut out the noise.

Here's how you can tap into focused energy and use it to increase your productivity, presence, and impact in every area of your life.

How to Apply Focused Energy

Focused energy isn't just about sitting in front of a task and hoping to be productive. It's about intentionally directing your energy in one direction and eliminating everything else that could distract you. It's an active process that requires mental discipline and the ability to shut down distractions. Here's how to cultivate and project focused energy:

Step 1: Recall a Time of High Focus

The first step in cultivating focused energy is to tap into a memory where you experienced laser-like concentration. Think of a time when you were working on a project, studying for an exam, or involved in a task that required your full attention. You may have felt completely immersed in the work, almost losing track of time, as if nothing could pull you away from the task at hand.

Maybe it was a time when you worked for hours straight, achieving a goal or making significant progress without any interruptions. Recall the clarity, the drive, and the sense of accomplishment you felt in that moment. This is the energy of focus, and by bringing this memory into your awareness, you can reconnect with that state of mind.

Step 2: Visualize the Energy Moving from Your Heart to Your Third Eye

Now, take that focused energy you've recalled and imagine it moving from your heart up to your third eye, the area between your eyebrows. The heart is the center of your willpower, your motivation, and your personal energy, while the third eye represents clarity and insight.

As you visualize this energy moving upward, feel it filling you with a deep sense of focus, concentration, and mental clarity. Your heart is fueling the focus, and your third eye sharpens it. You're no longer distracted by the outside world; your entire being is aligned with the task at hand.

At this point, you're preparing your mind to be fully present and engaged. Your mind isn't wandering to the past or the future; it's fixed solely on the present task. You are grounded in the moment, and your focus is centered.

Step 3: Imagine the Energy Settling Into Your Eyes

Once the energy has moved to your third eye, allow it to settle into your eyes. This is where your focus becomes visible to others. Your eyes are often the first place people look when they seek your attention or gauge your seriousness. With focused energy, your eyes take on a sharp, unwavering quality.

Imagine that your gaze becomes laser-like, precise, and unwavering. When you look at something, your eyes don't wander. They lock onto the task with intention and clarity. This is the energy that allows you to read deeply, work without distraction, and take on difficult tasks with confidence. When your gaze is aligned with your focus, you give off an impression of complete presence and determination.

Step 4: Direct That Focused Energy Toward the Task at Hand

Now that you've cultivated focused energy, it's time to direct it toward the task you want to accomplish. Whether you're writing a report, solving a complex problem, studying for an exam, or engaging in any task that requires deep focus, you need to pour all your attention and energy into it.

Visualize that focused energy extending outward from your eyes and infusing the task with your complete presence. If you're writing, imagine your focus directly flowing into the words, making them clearer and more impactful.

If you're brainstorming or problem-solving, picture your focused energy breaking through any barriers, unlocking creative solutions.

For example, if you're working on a project with tight deadlines, focus your energy on one step at a time. Instead of feeling overwhelmed by the whole project, break it down into smaller, manageable tasks and direct your full attention to each one. This step-by-step, concentrated approach allows you to make real progress without feeling distracted or pulled in too many directions.

If you're in a meeting or conversation where focus is required, direct your attention solely to the people and ideas in the room. Eliminate mental distractions and actively listen to what others are saying, staying present in the conversation. Your undivided attention will not only help you process the information better but will also make those around you feel respected and valued.

Step 5: Whisper to Yourself: "I Am Focused"

The final step is to affirm your ability to focus. As you're diving into the task or situation, whisper to yourself: "I am focused." This simple affirmation reinforces your state of mind and reminds you that you are in control. You are not a slave to distractions. You are in charge of where your attention goes.

By repeating this affirmation, you reprogram your mind to believe in your ability to maintain focus, even in challenging situations. Over time, this builds your internal capacity for focus and helps you become less susceptible to external distractions.

When to Use Focused Energy

Focused energy should be tapped into whenever you're faced with tasks or situations that require your full attention. It's particularly useful in the following scenarios:

Tackling Important Tasks

Whether you're working on a major project, writing a report, or preparing a presentation, focused energy is essential. When you need to dive deep into your work and accomplish something substantial, maintaining focus is key to getting results.

Example: Imagine you're working on an important presentation. If you allow your mind to wander, you might waste time on trivial matters, leaving the quality of the work compromised. By activating focused energy, you cut through distractions and create space to dive deep into the task. You're able to give the presentation your best work, ensuring a polished, impactful outcome.

Blocking Out Distractions

In the age of constant notifications, emails, and messages, it's easy to become overwhelmed by external distractions. Focused energy is the antidote. By tuning out the noise and directing all of your attention toward what you're doing, you can maximize your productivity and effectiveness.

Example: Suppose you're working from home, and distractions are everywhere: children, noise from other rooms, or your phone constantly buzzing. By applying focused energy, you can mentally block out everything but the task at hand. You give your attention to the work, putting your phone on silent, closing unnecessary tabs on your computer, and creating a space where you can concentrate fully.

Deep Problem-Solving or Creative Thinking

When you need to solve a complex problem or come up with new ideas, focused energy is essential. It allows you to shut down the noise and think clearly. Whether you're strategizing for business or working on a creative project, being able to focus all your mental power on the challenge in front of you will result in more innovative solutions and breakthrough thinking.

Example: You're working on a new product idea, and the solution isn't immediately apparent. By focusing your energy, you allow your mind to fully engage in creative thinking. Without distractions, you're able to explore different avenues, make connections, and arrive at a breakthrough idea.

Focused energy is the cornerstone of productivity, creativity, and achievement. It's not just about getting things done; it's about doing them with precision, clarity, and intent. By cultivating and projecting focused energy, you enhance your ability to perform at the highest level, block out distractions, and tackle challenges head-on. Focused energy allows you to be fully present in every situation, ensuring that your mental power is directed toward what matters most.

To harness this energy, all it takes is intention, practice, and mental discipline. Once you master focused energy, there will be no task too difficult, no challenge too great. You'll be able to move through the world with a sense of purpose, accomplishing your goals with precision and power. Get started today, and see how focused energy transforms your work, your mindset, and your life.

Visionary Energy: Igniting Bold Ideas and Inspiring Change

Visionary energy is the pulse of innovation and transformative thinking. It's the drive that allows you to see beyond the present moment, beyond what is, and into what could be. This energy is what sets leaders, entrepreneurs, and trailblazers apart from the rest. It's not just about having a good idea — it's about seeing the bigger picture, articulating it clearly, and motivating others to follow you on the journey toward that vision.

Visionary energy is the force that powers game-changing movements, revolutions in thought, and new ways of doing things. It's about sparking imagination, breaking the boundaries of what's possible, and daring to see the world not just as it is, but as it *could* be. And the best part? Visionary energy isn't reserved for a select few; anyone can tap into it and cultivate it to drive change and make an impact.

When you harness visionary energy, you don't just think about the next step — you think about the next *giant leap*. You see opportunities where others see obstacles, and you inspire those around you to believe in what they can't yet see.

Here's how to access and apply visionary energy to fuel your creativity, inspire others, and lead with a sense of purpose and possibility.

How to Apply Visionary Energy

To activate visionary energy, you need to connect with both your inner sense of possibility and your ability to communicate that vision to others. Visionary energy is about clarity, excitement, and boldness. It's about creating a narrative that paints a picture of what could be and convincing others to step into that future with you. Here's how to tap into this energy:

Step 1: Recall a Time When You Felt Visionary

Start by thinking back to a time when you felt visionary — a moment when you were working on something new, innovative, or transformative. This could be a time when you created a solution others didn't see, or when you came up with a bold idea that sparked change. It could be a time when you saw a problem and immediately began thinking of ways to solve it, or when you envisioned a future that others couldn't yet imagine.

For example, maybe it was a time when you were developing a business plan that could revolutionize an industry, or when you proposed a new project at work that had the potential to disrupt the status quo. Perhaps it was when you launched a new initiative, convinced others of its value, and saw it grow into something bigger than you originally imagined. Recall the excitement, the clarity, and the boldness you felt in that moment.

By reconnecting with that energy, you're grounding yourself in the sense of possibility and confidence that fuels visionary thinking.

Step 2: Visualize This Energy Rising from Your Heart to Your Third Eye

Now, take that visionary energy and imagine it rising from your heart — the seat of your passion and purpose — to your third eye, the center of intuition, insight, and higher thinking. Feel that energy move upwards, filling you with a sense of clarity, purpose, and deep understanding of what could be possible.

As the energy moves from your heart to your third eye, let it amplify your sense of vision. Imagine it expanding your ability to see not just the present moment, but the potential of every situation, every project, and every relationship. When visionary energy is activated, you begin to see what others may overlook — the opportunities, the trends, the gaps, and the innovations that could drive change.

This step is about sharpening your ability to "see" your ideas. It's about cultivating an inner sight that allows you to see far beyond the immediate and the tangible, and focus on what could emerge.

Step 3: Imagine the Energy Flowing Outward Through Your Eyes

Once the visionary energy has filled your heart and mind, imagine it flowing outward through your eyes. Your eyes become the conduit through which you transmit your vision to the world. As you look at people or a group, you are no longer just seeing them — you are transmitting your ideas, your vision, and your excitement for what's possible.

This is where you start to speak and act with clarity and conviction. Your eyes lock onto others with purpose. You're no longer just talking about the present situation; you're showing them the future — the direction that excites you and where you want to go. When you speak about your vision, others are drawn to it because they see the passion and excitement in your gaze. You are radiating the energy of possibility.

Step 4: Send That Energy to People or Groups You Want to Inspire

Now that you've cultivated visionary energy within yourself, it's time to direct it toward others. Visualize sending this energy to the people or groups who you want to inspire or influence. Whether you're speaking to a team, presenting in front of a room, or having a one-on-one conversation, send that energy toward them with the intent of sparking their imagination, inspiring action, and getting them to buy into the big picture.

If you're brainstorming with a team, imagine the visionary energy flowing between you and your colleagues, amplifying creativity and expanding everyone's capacity to think beyond the conventional. In a meeting, send this energy to your audience to encourage them to adopt a fresh perspective and get behind your ideas.

Example: Imagine you're pitching a new idea to a group of investors. As you speak, you direct your visionary energy toward them, engaging them with your clarity, excitement, and belief in what your idea can become. Instead of just explaining the features of your product, you articulate a vision for how it will change the market, improve lives, or disrupt an entire industry. Your energy draws them in, and your words paint a picture of what's possible, leaving them inspired and excited about the future.

Step 5: Whisper to Yourself: "I Am Visionary"

The final step is to affirm your visionary power. Whisper to yourself: "I am visionary." This statement reinforces your belief in your ability to think big, see the future, and inspire others to take action. As you say this, feel the energy of your vision growing stronger within you. You are a creator, a forward-thinker, a person who doesn't just wait for change — you *make* it happen.

By repeating this mantra, you solidify your identity as a visionary. This affirmation shifts your mindset, keeps you aligned with your long-term goals, and ensures that your vision will continue to evolve. The more you practice this, the more natural visionary energy will become for you.

When to Use Visionary Energy

Visionary energy is essential whenever you're looking to inspire others, lead with foresight, or make something extraordinary happen. Here are a few key times to activate it:

During Brainstorming or Innovation Meetings

Whenever you're involved in creative collaborations or discussions about new ideas, visionary energy is your best friend. It allows you to think expansively and see connections and possibilities that others might not notice. It helps you step beyond conventional thinking and tap into innovative, future-focused ideas.

Example: In a team meeting where you're tasked with developing new marketing strategies, your visionary energy helps you see an uncharted direction — one that others might overlook. You bring fresh ideas to the table, challenge existing assumptions, and show your team how they can think beyond the immediate, tapping into a future vision that excites everyone.

When Influencing Others to Embrace a New Direction

Whether you're leading a company, rallying a group, or attempting to drive change, visionary energy is essential when you want to influence others to embrace new ideas or directions. It's about convincing people to take the leap into the unknown and trust in a future they can't yet fully see.

Example: If you're leading a company through a period of transformation, your visionary energy helps you present a compelling case for why the changes are necessary and how they will benefit everyone in the long run. You paint a picture of the company's future, one that's thriving and innovative, and draw people into that vision.

Anytime You Need to Convey Big-Picture Thinking or Strategy

Visionary energy is also critical in strategic planning. Whether you're mapping out a long-term business plan, designing a new product, or even planning a personal project, visionary energy allows you to think strategically about the future and communicate that vision to others.

Example: If you're planning a new product launch, visionary energy helps you see the big picture: not just how the product will function, but how it will change the market, how it will grow your brand, and how it will impact your customers. By tapping into this energy, you're able to create a narrative around your product that excites people, investors, and customers alike.

Visionary energy is the fuel for bold ideas, innovative thinking, and transformative leadership. It's what allows you to see beyond the limits of today and imagine a world that others might not yet believe is possible. By cultivating and projecting visionary energy, you can inspire others, lead change, and take action toward creating a future that aligns with your boldest dreams.

Visionary energy is not just for a select few — it's for anyone who dares to dream, who dares to see beyond the horizon. Activate it, harness it, and watch as you transform your vision into reality.

Playful Energy: Lighten the Mood and Build Connection

Playful energy is the type of charisma that makes people smile, laugh, and feel at ease. It's that infectious energy that can defuse tension, break the ice, and bring a sense of joy to any interaction. Whether it's a casual conversation or a high-stakes meeting, playful energy has the power to create a relaxed atmosphere where people feel comfortable and open. When you embody this energy, you don't just lighten the room — you lighten everyone's mood. People are drawn to you because of the fun, spontaneous, and playful vibe you project.

Playful energy is not about being immature or childish. It's about having a light-hearted, carefree attitude that brings a sense of joy and spontaneity to your interactions. This type of charisma invites people to be themselves, relax their guard, and engage with you in a more authentic, enjoyable way.

Now, let's explore how to access and apply playful energy in various situations, so you can connect with others, lighten the mood, and have a good time while doing it.

How to Apply Playful Energy

To access playful energy, you must first reconnect with the playful, carefree part of yourself — the part that knows how to enjoy life and have fun, no matter the circumstances. Playful energy requires you to let go of rigid control, embrace spontaneity, and inject fun into your interactions. Here's how to bring it to life:

Step 1: Recall a Time When You Felt Carefree and Playful

Start by thinking back to a time when you felt genuinely playful. This could be a time you were out with friends, engaging in a spontaneous adventure, or even when you were caught in an unexpected moment of laughter. Maybe it was during a vacation, a fun outing with your family, or even a moment when you were just hanging out with someone and didn't have a care in the world.

Recalling this moment helps you tap into the positive, fun-loving energy you felt then. Reconnect with the joy, the lightness, and the feeling of having no pressure. Let this memory flood your mind, and feel the joy of it in your body. Remember how it felt to just be in the moment without trying to impress anyone or overthink things.

Example: Maybe you remember a time you went on a spontaneous road trip with friends, driving down a winding highway, laughing about silly things, singing along to your favorite tunes. The carefree nature of that experience is your entry point to playful energy.

Step 2: Visualize This Playful Energy Filling Your Heart

Once you've recalled a time when you felt playful and joyful, imagine that energy moving from your mind to your heart. See it as a warm, glowing light — something vibrant and full of energy. Visualize that light expanding as it fills your entire chest, making you feel lighthearted, free, and full of energy.

As you do this, let that warmth spread throughout your body. Feel your shoulders relax, your muscles loosen, and a sense of joy begin to bubble up inside you. This step is about reconnecting with your inner playfulness — the part of you that loves to enjoy life and doesn't take things too seriously.

Step 3: Let the Playful Energy Rise to Your Third Eye and Spread Through Your Eyes

Now that the playful energy has settled in your heart, let it rise to your third eye — the center of insight and imagination. Picture the energy moving upward, filling you with a sense of clarity and vision. Then, let this energy spill outward through your eyes, causing your gaze to become lighter, more relaxed, and full of playful energy.

Imagine that your eyes are sparkling with enthusiasm, as if you're ready to share a joke or light-hearted comment. Your expression becomes more animated, your face more inviting, and your body more relaxed. The playful energy in your eyes invites others to engage with you, as they feel the fun and ease radiating from your gaze.

Example: When you speak to someone, imagine your eyes twinkling as you tell a light-hearted story, causing them to smile or laugh along with you. Your playful energy will make them feel more relaxed and comfortable, drawing them into your presence.

Step 4: Send This Energy to People Around You

Now, direct this playful energy toward the people around you. Whether you're in a casual conversation, a meeting, or a social gathering, visualize your playful energy flowing outward and lightening the mood. Imagine it spreading through the space, making people feel at ease and inviting them to engage in a more relaxed and enjoyable way.

In a meeting, for example, you might use playful energy to break the tension when the atmosphere feels a little too serious. A quick joke, a playful comment, or even just a relaxed, smiling demeanor can shift the energy in the room. This allows people to drop their guard, feel more connected, and even open up creatively.

Example: In a social gathering where the conversation is stiff, inject a little humor. Maybe you share a funny anecdote, or playfully tease someone in a lighthearted way. This helps ease any tension, and soon, others will start to join in with their own playful energy, creating a more comfortable and enjoyable atmosphere for everyone.

Step 5: Whisper to Yourself: "I Am Playful"

Finally, reinforce your playful energy with a simple affirmation: "I am playful." This is a way to ground yourself in this energy and remind yourself that you have the power to bring lightness and fun to any situation. As you whisper this affirmation, feel the sense of joy and ease spreading through you, solidifying your connection to your playful side.

This step is crucial because it helps you internalize your playful energy. Whenever you feel yourself becoming too serious or tense, simply repeat this affirmation to return to a more relaxed, fun-loving mindset. Over time, the more you practice this, the easier it will become to tap into your playful energy whenever you need it.

Example: In a moment of stress, take a deep breath and repeat, "I am playful." Let go of the tension and see the humor in the situation. Instead of getting stuck in the stress, you shift your energy to something more light-hearted, allowing you to handle challenges with ease and grace.

When to Use Playful Energy

Playful energy is incredibly versatile and can be applied in a wide variety of situations. Here are some key times when tapping into playful energy can be especially useful:

When You Need to Break the Ice in a Tense Situation

If you find yourself in a high-stakes or tense situation, playful energy can be your secret weapon to ease the tension. Whether it's a tough negotiation, a high-pressure meeting, or an awkward social encounter, a little humor or lightness can break the ice and help everyone feel more at ease.

Example: In a business meeting where people seem nervous or uptight, you might make a self-deprecating joke or share a funny story to lighten the mood. This can quickly change the tone of the room, helping everyone to relax and communicate more effectively.

When You Want to Create a Fun, Relaxed Atmosphere

Playful energy is perfect for setting a light, enjoyable atmosphere, whether it's a team-building event, a social gathering, or a casual hangout with friends. If things are feeling too stiff, you can use playful energy to encourage others to loosen up and have fun.

Example: At a dinner party, you might use playful energy to get people talking and laughing. Whether it's telling a funny story or joking around with people, your playful attitude will help others feel more comfortable and open up, creating a fun atmosphere where everyone can enjoy themselves.

Anytime You Want to Connect with Others in a Light-Hearted Way

Playful energy is ideal for creating connections with others. If you want to make people feel comfortable and get them to open up, bring some playful energy into your interactions. When people feel like they can relax and enjoy themselves around you, they'll be more likely to engage and bond with you.

Example: If you're meeting someone new, a little humor can go a long way in making them feel at ease. A playful comment or a funny observation about the situation can instantly connect you and create a friendly, relaxed dynamic.

Playful energy is the charisma that brings joy, laughter, and ease into any interaction. It's about being light-hearted, spontaneous, and able to create an atmosphere of fun and connection. By applying playful energy in the right moments, you can break tension, foster creativity, and build stronger relationships. Whether you're leading a team, networking at a party, or just chatting with a friend, playful energy helps you connect with others in a way that feels effortless, authentic, and enjoyable.

So, tap into your playful side. Don't be afraid to let loose, crack a joke, or enjoy the moment. Playful energy is contagious — the more you exude it, the more it will spread. And when you do, people will feel lighter, more engaged, and more drawn to your presence.

Remember:

The beauty of the Charisma Activity lies in its versatility: it allows you to tap into and project any type of energy that serves you best in any given situation. Charisma is not a fixed trait — it's a skill that can be developed, refined, and adjusted to fit your needs. By consciously harnessing and channeling specific energies like **confidence**, **compassion**, **leadership**, **focus**, **vision**, or **playfulness**, you can enhance your presence, magnetism, and influence in a variety of contexts.

Here's how it works:

- **Confidence** lets you command attention and assert yourself with self-assurance.
- **Compassion** creates deep connections, fostering trust and empathy with others.
- **Leadership** enables you to inspire, motivate, and guide people toward a shared goal.
- **Focused Energy** sharpens your attention, allowing you to handle tasks with precision and clarity.
- **Visionary Energy** helps you see the bigger picture, inspiring others with bold ideas and future-thinking.
- **Playful Energy** breaks tension, brings joy, and makes you approachable in any setting.

By practicing the Charisma Activity regularly, these energies become ingrained in your persona. Over time, you'll be able to seamlessly shift between them, adjusting your presence to meet the demands of each moment. Whether you're leading a team, navigating a difficult conversation, brainstorming ideas, or simply socializing, you'll find that your ability to influence and connect with others becomes effortless.

The result? You'll handle every situation with **grace**, **ease**, and **magnetic influence**. Charisma, once a distant or intangible quality, will become a natural extension of who you are, allowing you to leave a lasting impression wherever you go.

So, practice. Commit to using these energies every day. The more you engage with them, the more they'll become second nature — a toolkit of charisma that you can wield with precision and power. The world will take notice.

Perfect Thought Extension: The Perfect Space

Embracing Challenging Locations

The **Perfect Space Activity** is a tool designed to help you embrace and transform uncomfortable or challenging environments into opportunities for growth. Whether you find yourself in a stressful meeting, a crowded place, or an emotionally charged situation, this activity teaches you to shift from resistance and frustration to acceptance and calm.

Key Steps in the Perfect Space Activity:

- **Acknowledge Your Current Space**
  - Begin by acknowledging the environment you're in, whether physical, emotional, or mental. Instead of resisting or judging it, simply observe and accept your reality.
  - **Example**: In a tense meeting, instead of reacting with frustration, recognize you're in this space and it's exactly where you need to be.

- **Shift from Resistance to Acceptance**
  - Let go of any resistance and accept the situation as it is. Understand that discomfort isn't an enemy but a teacher that offers an opportunity for growth.
  - **Example**: Stuck in traffic? Accept that it's part of the situation and choose how to respond—use the time productively or calmly.

- **Reframe the Space as Perfect for Your Growth**
  - See every space, even a difficult one, as an opportunity to learn and grow. Ask yourself: *What can I learn from this?*
  - **Example**: In a high-pressure work environment, consider what the situation can teach you—patience, leadership, or time management.

- **Use the Space to Center Yourself**
  - Focus on calming techniques, like deep breathing, to center yourself. This allows you to maintain peace and clarity, regardless of the external chaos.
  - **Example**: In an argument, focus on your breath to stay

grounded and respond thoughtfully instead of reacting emotionally.

- **Embrace the Space as a Tool for Growth**
  - Every situation, even if uncomfortable, is a tool for personal growth. Embrace challenges with curiosity and view them as opportunities to build resilience, patience, and other qualities.
  - **Example**: A project not going well? See it as a chance to refine problem-solving skills or ask for support.

When to Use the Perfect Space Activity:

- **Stressful work situations** like high-pressure meetings or tight deadlines.
- **Emotionally charged moments** like arguments or personal conflict.
- **Uncomfortable physical spaces** like crowded places or waiting rooms.
- **Situations that trigger anxiety or frustration**, helping you reframe them as opportunities for personal growth.

The Perfect Space Activity is about transforming discomfort into self-mastery. By acknowledging, accepting, and reframing any environment as perfect for growth, you can find peace and presence in any situation. Regular practice helps you embrace challenges and use them as tools for learning and personal evolution.

Why the Perfect Space?

We all have those spaces—physical locations or emotional environments—that stir up discomfort, unease, or negative emotions. You know the ones I'm talking about. Maybe it's a particular room in your house that holds memories of past conflict or loss. Maybe it's a place at work that triggers feelings of inadequacy or stress. Or perhaps it's a social setting that reminds you of failure, rejection, or vulnerability. These spaces don't just occupy physical space—they often occupy mental and emotional space, too, affecting how we feel and behave when we encounter them.

The truth is, these "trigger spaces" are unavoidable. They're part of life. We all experience them. Whether it's a physical location, a situation that brings up anxiety, or a mental space we enter when faced with stress, we can't avoid these uncomfortable moments. But here's the twist: we don't have to be victims of these spaces. We can *choose* how to engage with them. And that's where the **Perfect Space Activity** comes in.

The core purpose of this activity is to help you shift your perception of those challenging spaces. Instead of avoiding them, resenting them, or letting them overwhelm you, the goal is to *embrace* them. That's right—embrace discomfort, frustration, or even fear. Sounds counterintuitive, right? But here's the thing: this doesn't mean pretending that everything is okay or ignoring the emotional weight these spaces might carry. It's about recognizing that, no matter how uncomfortable the space is, there's something valuable in it. Whether it's a lesson, an opportunity, or a moment for personal growth, every space has something to offer if you approach it with the right mindset.

The Power of Perception

How you perceive a space dictates how you experience it. For instance, if you walk into a room where you've faced failure in the past, the feeling of failure may resurface immediately. But if you shift your perspective, you can view that space not as a reminder of past shortcomings, but as a symbol of growth. After all, you've learned from those failures, and that room can now serve as a place of reflection, not regret. It's a place where you can witness your own evolution.

The Perfect Space Activity challenges the typical human response to stressful or triggering environments: **avoidance** or **resistance**. Instead of rejecting uncomfortable spaces or trying to escape them, this activity encourages you to lean into them, to fully experience them with the understanding that they are part of your journey. Rather than seeing the space as an obstacle, it becomes a vehicle for self-discovery and growth.

For example, consider a situation where you walk into a meeting that you've dreaded, perhaps because you've faced criticism in that space before. If you let the history of that space dictate your feelings, it will control you. But if you can shift your mindset to view it as an opportunity to improve your emotional resilience, practice your communication skills, or even redefine how you handle conflict, then that meeting becomes a space of personal growth, not a space of fear.

The Challenge of Resistance

Here's the crux of the matter: **resistance is the root of suffering**. When we resist the space we're in—whether it's an uncomfortable room, an emotionally charged situation, or an environment that makes us feel powerless—we only create more discomfort for ourselves. This resistance magnifies negative emotions like frustration, anxiety, and helplessness.

Think about it. When you resist a difficult situation, you focus all your energy on wishing things were different. You're not allowing yourself to be present. You're stuck in a mental battle with the environment, and that only drains your energy and peace of mind.

In contrast, when you accept the space you're in, you stop fighting against the current. Acceptance doesn't mean liking or endorsing what's happening; it simply means acknowledging that this is the space you are in at this moment, and it has something to offer you.

The Lesson of Embracing Challenging Spaces

By embracing challenging spaces, you create the mental and emotional freedom to navigate them more effectively. You don't need to be held captive by the discomfort. Instead, you can learn how to *move through it* with calmness, grace, and an open heart. When you stop resisting, you give yourself the chance to access your full potential—your resilience, your problem-solving ability, your creativity, and your strength.

This doesn't mean that difficult spaces won't bring up negative emotions. Of course, they will. The goal isn't to suppress those feelings; the goal is to allow them to exist *without letting them control you*.

Let's break it down with some examples:

- **Public Speaking**: If you've ever been asked to speak in front of a group, you know the discomfort that can arise. You might feel anxiety, fear of judgment, or imposter syndrome. Rather than fighting these feelings, embrace the space. Acknowledge that the nervousness is normal, and see it as a sign that you care. Recognize that this moment is an opportunity to practice confidence, communicate clearly, and develop your public speaking skills. The more you embrace these moments, the more comfortable you'll become with public speaking.

- **Conflict in Relationships**: We all encounter challenging conversations with loved ones. Whether it's a disagreement or a difficult conversation, these spaces can trigger deep emotional reactions. Rather than avoiding the conversation or letting it spiral into frustration, lean into the discomfort. Recognize that conflict often brings clarity, understanding, and deeper connection. See the space as an opportunity to improve your communication, set boundaries, and foster mutual respect.

- **Professional Challenges**: You might find yourself in a high-pressure situation at work—whether it's a big project with tight deadlines or a difficult negotiation. These spaces often evoke stress or anxiety. Instead of resisting the pressure, accept that this challenge is here to help you grow. It's pushing you to innovate, manage stress, and find solutions under pressure. Embrace it as an opportunity to demonstrate leadership, resilience, and problem-solving skills.

- **Personal Growth**: There are times when the space you're in isn't external but internal. Perhaps you're experiencing doubt or fear about your own potential. These internal "spaces" of negative self-talk can be some of the most challenging. Instead of rejecting or running away from these emotions, see them as opportunities to practice self-compassion, to challenge limiting beliefs, and to strengthen your mindset.

The Power of Acceptance

The Perfect Space Activity is a reminder that *every space*—whether it's physical, emotional, or mental—is perfect for your growth. The discomfort, the challenges, and the struggles are not obstacles to avoid; they are invitations to expand and evolve. When you embrace the space you're in, you stop being controlled by your surroundings. You take control of your emotional state, your thoughts, and ultimately, your life.

So, the next time you find yourself in a challenging space, whether it's a stressful situation or an uncomfortable environment, try the Perfect Space

Activity. Instead of resisting, lean into the discomfort. Acknowledge that this space is offering you exactly what you need to grow. With practice, you'll find that no matter where you are—physically, mentally, or emotionally—you can always find peace, presence, and purpose.

How to Practice the Perfect Space Activity

The **Perfect Space Activity** is all about shifting your perception of discomfort and turning challenging environments into opportunities for personal growth. Whether you're in a physical space that makes you anxious or a mental or emotional state that feels stuck or overwhelming, this activity helps you embrace the moment and transform it into something constructive. Below is a step-by-step guide on how to practice the Perfect Space Activity, along with examples to help you visualize each step:

Identify the Troubling Space

The first step is to pinpoint a space—whether physical, emotional, or mental—that brings up feelings of discomfort, stress, or unease. This might be a room or environment, a specific situation, or even a state of mind that you tend to avoid or react negatively to.

Examples of Troubling Spaces:

- **Physical Spaces:**
    - Your office, where you feel overwhelmed by work demands or underappreciated.
    - A doctor's office that triggers anxiety about health or past traumatic medical experiences.
    - A place from your childhood that brings up painful memories.
- **Emotional Spaces:**
    - Family gatherings where old tensions or unresolved conflicts surface.
    - Situations that trigger feelings of helplessness, rejection, or judgment.
- **Mental Spaces:**
    - A feeling of being stuck or lost, where you feel unsure about your next step in life or career.

   ○ Overthinking or spiraling thoughts that cloud your clarity and peace.

The key here is to *identify* where your resistance lies. Recognizing the troubling space is half the battle. Once you know what triggers you, you can start to work with it.

Pause and Breathe

Now that you've identified the space, the next step is to pause. Take a moment to ground yourself and return to the present. This helps interrupt the automatic response of resistance or anxiety that often accompanies these spaces.

How to do it:

- **Deep Breathing**: Close your eyes, place your feet flat on the ground, and take a few deep, calming breaths. As you breathe in, imagine drawing in peace and clarity. As you exhale, release any tension or negative emotion tied to the space.
- **Physical Grounding**: Feel your feet pressing against the floor. Visualize roots extending down from your body into the earth, connecting you to the present moment. This helps calm your nervous system and center your mind.
- **Mindful Awareness**: Focus on your breathing, and with each inhale, try to release any judgment or resistance to the space you're in. Don't rush—just focus on being present.

Affirm the Space

This is the turning point in the Perfect Space Activity. You're going to affirm that *this* space—no matter how uncomfortable—is exactly where you need to be right now. This affirmation shifts your mindset from resistance to acceptance.

How to do it:

- **Mental Affirmation**: Quietly say to yourself, "This space is perfect now." Feel the weight of those words settle into your being.
  - ○ You're not saying that everything in the space is ideal, but

you're acknowledging that this space—difficult, uncomfortable, or triggering as it may be—is offering you exactly what you need at this moment.

- **Non-Resistance**: The goal here isn't to force yourself to love the space or to pretend it's comfortable, but rather to accept it as it is, in this very moment. Recognizing that each space, no matter how uncomfortable, holds the potential for growth or learning, helps reduce mental resistance.

Example:

- If you're in a high-pressure work meeting that usually triggers anxiety, you could affirm to yourself, "This moment is exactly what I need to grow. I am here to learn how to handle pressure with calm." By shifting your mental focus from dread to growth, you reframe the experience.

Notice the Shift

As you repeat the affirmation and allow it to settle into your consciousness, observe what begins to shift within you. You might not feel an immediate sense of ease, but the act of accepting the space allows you to release some of your mental and emotional resistance.

How to notice the shift:

- **Physical Relaxation**: You may begin to notice that your body starts to relax. Perhaps your shoulders drop, your breathing becomes deeper, and your muscles loosen. This is a physical sign that you are letting go of tension.
- **Mental Shift**: Your thoughts might change from negative or judgmental to neutral or positive. Instead of thinking, "I hate being here," you might notice your thoughts shift to, "I am here, and I can handle this."
- **Emotional Calm**: You may still feel discomfort, but it will feel less intense. Instead of feeling overwhelmed or trapped, you'll notice a

sense of inner calm settling over you. This is the power of acceptance at work.

Example:

- If you're at a family gathering where past tensions always arise, the affirmation "This space is perfect now" might initially feel strange, but over time you may begin to feel more open, less defensive, and less reactive to old triggers. Your emotional reaction might soften, allowing you to engage with others more calmly.

Engage with the Space

Now that you've accepted the space, it's time to engage with it in a way that helps you remain present, grounded, and at peace. This step involves interacting with the space—not avoiding it, but embracing it with awareness.

How to do it:

- **For Physical Spaces**: Pay attention to the details of your environment. Notice the sights, sounds, and smells around you. This helps to pull you into the present moment rather than being lost in worry or discomfort.
    - For instance, if you're in a crowded room that typically causes anxiety, focus on the physical sensations. Feel the chair beneath you, the air around you, the people nearby. Take in the details and remind yourself that you are safe, right here and right now.
- **For Emotional Spaces**: If you're experiencing intense emotions, allow yourself to feel them without judgment. Acknowledge what's happening within you, whether it's fear, sadness, or frustration. Say to yourself, "It's okay to feel this right now. I'm learning how to stay calm in this moment."
    - For example, if you're experiencing frustration during a difficult conversation, acknowledge your irritation, but instead of letting it take over, consciously choose to remain present and open.

- **For Mental Spaces**: If your mind is racing with worries, gently redirect your thoughts. Focus on your breathing, your immediate surroundings, or the task at hand. If you feel lost or unsure about what's next, reassure yourself: "I am exactly where I need to be. I am open to learning from this moment."
  - For example, if you're facing uncertainty about your career or life path, instead of becoming overwhelmed by doubt, focus on the next small step you can take. Acknowledge the uncertainty as part of your journey.

The **Perfect Space Activity** is an empowering practice that helps you shift from resistance to acceptance in challenging environments. By embracing rather than avoiding the discomfort of these spaces, you open yourself up to learning, growth, and deeper resilience. Every space—whether physical, emotional, or mental—holds potential for insight, and through practice, you can train yourself to find peace and acceptance in any situation.

With consistent practice, this activity helps you navigate life with greater ease, confidence, and a deeper understanding that every space, no matter how challenging, is perfect for your growth.

8 Common "Troubling Space" Scenarios

The **Perfect Space Activity** can be particularly helpful when navigating challenging or uncomfortable environments. Whether it's a physical space, an emotional space, or even a mental space that triggers discomfort, this activity helps you shift from resistance to acceptance. Here are **8 common troubling space scenarios** and how you can use the Perfect Space Mindset to turn these situations into opportunities for growth.

The Office or Workplace

Scenario:

You walk into your office or a meeting, and immediately feel overwhelmed by the workload, stressed by looming deadlines, or judged by colleagues. The atmosphere feels heavy, and you're consumed with anxiety about how you're being perceived.

Perfect Space Mindset:

"This space is perfect now."

What to Do:

- **Pause and Breathe**: Take a deep breath and focus on grounding yourself. Feel the tension in your shoulders and consciously release it.
- **Reframe the Situation**: Remind yourself that you're in this space to learn and grow. Use this opportunity to practice patience, improve communication skills, or resolve conflicts.
- **Mindful Engagement**: Instead of being swept up by the stress, engage with your tasks one by one. Prioritize what needs attention first and tackle challenges with a calm and open mind.

A Doctor's Office or Hospital

Scenario:

You're sitting in a sterile doctor's office, or perhaps you're waiting for test results, and the anticipation of bad news creates a sense of anxiety or fear. The environment itself feels cold and unsettling.

Perfect Space Mindset:

"This space is perfect now."

What to Do:

- **Acknowledge Fear**: Recognize the fear, but don't let it consume you. It's okay to be anxious, but don't let the anxiety control you.
- **Focus on Breathing**: Breathe deeply to calm your nervous system. Inhale peace, exhale fear.
- **Shift Your Focus to Self-Care**: Remind yourself that you are in this space because you are actively taking care of your health, which is a positive step in itself.

Home During Family Conflict

Scenario:

Family conflicts create a charged, emotionally intense atmosphere in your home. Old issues resurface, and the environment becomes tense, causing discomfort or stress.

Perfect Space Mindset:

"This space is perfect now."
What to Do:

- **Practice Mindfulness**: Take a step back and acknowledge your emotions without judgment. Feel the discomfort, but don't let it control your response.
- **Active Listening**: Use the situation as an opportunity to listen more deeply, communicate with empathy, or take space if necessary.
- **Embrace Compassion**: Recognize that conflict is a natural part of relationships and use this as an opportunity for healing and growth within the family.

Public Spaces (e.g., Airports, Crowded Streets)

Scenario:

You're in a crowded public space, such as an airport or on a busy street, and the noise, chaos, and sheer number of people overwhelm you. The clutter of activity creates a sense of discomfort or even anxiety.

Perfect Space Mindset:

"This space is perfect now."

What to Do:

- **Focus on Sensory Details**: Shift your focus from the overwhelming environment to sensory details. What can you see, hear, or smell around you?
- **Breathe and Stay Present**: Instead of wishing for the crowd to dissipate, breathe deeply and embrace the activity. Find calm within the chaos by focusing on the present moment.
- **Embrace the Flow**: View the activity around you as part of the natural ebb and flow of life. Instead of feeling overwhelmed, practice remaining centered in the midst of external noise.

Places of Emotional Pain (e.g., Former Homes, Locations Linked to Loss)

Scenario:

You return to a location tied to past trauma, loss, or painful memories (e.g., a former home, a place where you experienced heartbreak). The place triggers feelings of sadness, regret, or emotional discomfort.

Perfect Space Mindset:

"This space is perfect now."

What to Do:

- **Acknowledge the Memories**: Recognize the emotions that arise. It's natural to feel sadness, anger, or grief, but don't let those feelings dictate how you respond.
- **Shift Your Focus**: Redirect your attention to the present moment. Reframe the space as an opportunity for healing, allowing yourself to be present with the emotions without becoming overwhelmed by them.
- **Create a New Meaning**: Use this space as a place for closure or acceptance, honoring the past while choosing to move forward with peace.

The Gym or Physical Training Space

Scenario:

You enter the gym or a physical training space and feel self-conscious, inadequate, or frustrated with your progress. The environment might feel intimidating, or you might compare yourself negatively to others.

Perfect Space Mindset:

"This space is perfect now."

What to Do:

- **Release Judgment**: Let go of any self-judgment or comparison. Recognize that everyone is on their own unique journey, and the gym is a place to improve yourself, not to compete with others.
- **Focus on Your Body**: Acknowledge your body and the positive steps you're taking to improve it. Embrace the discomfort as part of your growth.
- **Practice Patience**: Allow yourself to be present with your training.

Celebrate each small progress, knowing that the process itself is a victory.

During an Important Presentation or Speech

Scenario:

You're about to give a presentation or speech, and the nerves, self-doubt, or fear of judgment overwhelm you. The environment feels tense, and you're unsure of how you'll perform.

Perfect Space Mindset:

"This space is perfect now."

What to Do:

- **Use Nervous Energy**: Reframe your nervousness as energy that can fuel a powerful performance.
- **Shift Your Focus**: Instead of focusing on your fear of judgment, focus on the message you want to deliver. You're here to share something meaningful, and that's what matters.
- **Embrace the Moment**: Accept that nerves are a natural part of the process. Acknowledge the discomfort and move forward anyway, knowing that you have the power to handle it.

The Bedroom (When Sleep or Rest Feels Elusive)

Scenario:

You lie in bed, tossing and turning, unable to sleep. The more you try to force rest, the more frustrated you become, making the bedroom feel like a source of stress rather than relaxation.

Perfect Space Mindset:

"This space is perfect now."

What to Do:

- **Release Frustration**: Let go of the need to force sleep. Acknowledge the frustration but choose not to let it control your mind.
- **Practice Relaxation**: Engage in gentle relaxation techniques, such as deep breathing, progressive muscle relaxation, or visualization.

- **Embrace Rest**: Remember that rest doesn't always have to come in the form of sleep. Resting your mind and body in this moment is still valuable, even if sleep doesn't come right away.

The **Perfect Space Activity** can help you transform any environment—whether it's an office, a family home, or even a moment of personal discomfort—into an opportunity for growth and peace. By adopting the mindset that *"This space is perfect now,"* you move from resistance to acceptance, finding clarity, peace, and potential for growth in each experience. Whether it's facing your fears in a doctor's office or finding calm in a crowded airport, the Perfect Space Activity empowers you to engage with challenging environments in a balanced, empowered way.

The Benefits of the Perfect Space Activity

The **Perfect Space Activity** is a transformative practice designed to help you navigate and embrace challenging or uncomfortable environments, whether they are physical, emotional, or mental. The key benefit of this activity lies in its ability to shift your perception of any space from one of resistance to acceptance. By consistently practicing this mindset, you can transform negative or stressful situations into opportunities for personal growth and emotional resilience. Here are the core benefits of the Perfect Space Activity:

Reduced Resistance

One of the most significant benefits of the Perfect Space Activity is the reduction of **emotional resistance**. Often, when we find ourselves in uncomfortable or stressful environments, our instinct is to fight against it, wish for a different circumstance, or mentally escape. This resistance creates an internal conflict that can intensify stress, anxiety, and discomfort.

By consciously accepting the space you're in and embracing the idea that it is "perfect now," you immediately reduce that resistance. You stop wishing for the situation to change and, instead, open yourself to the present moment as it is. This shift from resistance to acceptance not only frees up mental energy but also helps you face challenges with a calm and open mindset. The less you resist, the less power the environment has over your emotional state.

Example:

In a tense work meeting, instead of mentally wishing to escape or change the situation, you choose to accept it as it is. This subtle shift allows you to be present, listen better, and contribute in a more grounded, productive way.

Emotional Growth

The Perfect Space Activity provides a unique opportunity for **emotional growth**. Life is full of situations that challenge our emotional resilience, whether it's a difficult conversation, a high-pressure work environment, or a place tied to painful memories. By learning to embrace these spaces, you grow emotionally and spiritually.

This practice teaches you to face uncomfortable emotions, accept them, and integrate the lessons they have to offer. Rather than avoiding or suppressing feelings, you acknowledge them, work through them, and emerge stronger and more self-aware.

Example:

Returning to a family home filled with memories of past struggles or trauma can trigger sadness or frustration. Rather than resisting these feelings, you use the Perfect Space Activity to accept the space as it is and find moments of growth within those emotions. This might mean offering yourself compassion or finding healing in the present moment, rather than being overwhelmed by the past.

Increased Presence

Another key benefit of the Perfect Space Activity is the **increased presence** it fosters. Whether you're at home, in a public space, or facing an emotionally charged environment, this practice helps you stay grounded in the present moment.

In today's fast-paced world, it's easy to get caught up in our thoughts and anxieties about the future or past. The more we dwell on what's not going well, the more disconnected we become from the present moment. The Perfect Space Activity encourages you to shift your attention from mental distractions to being fully aware of your environment and your experience within it.

When you learn to embrace a space instead of resisting it, you become more attuned to the sensations, feelings, and insights that arise in the present moment. Whether you're in a stressful situation or simply in a place you find uncomfortable, this practice helps you remain anchored, preventing you from being swept away by emotional or mental turmoil.

Example:

During a challenging conversation with a colleague or a family member, instead of ruminating over the conflict or worrying about how it will turn out, you use the Perfect Space mindset to stay present with the person and the conversation. This helps you listen more deeply, respond more thoughtfully, and engage with the situation in a way that fosters connection rather than escalation.

Stress Reduction

The Perfect Space Activity significantly aids in **stress reduction**. Stress often arises when we try to control or change our environment, especially when we feel trapped in situations we perceive as less than ideal. We spend energy fighting against the circumstances, which only intensifies the stress and anxiety.

By accepting that the space you are in is exactly where you need to be right now, you release the urge to control or change your environment. This reduces the internal tension and creates a sense of calm. When you stop resisting, the external environment has less power over your internal state, and your ability to handle stress improves.

Additionally, practicing acceptance in difficult spaces can help you break the cycle of rumination, which is often a contributor to chronic stress. The act of affirming that "this space is perfect now" shifts your focus away from what's wrong and instead helps you find peace in what is.

Example:

Imagine you are stuck in traffic, late for an important meeting. The initial impulse might be to become frustrated or anxious. Instead, by embracing the Perfect Space Activity, you shift your mindset, accept the situation as it is, and use the time in traffic as an opportunity to breathe deeply, listen to music, or calm your mind, reducing the stress that might otherwise arise from the situation.

At its core, the **Perfect Space Activity** is about **embracing the spaces in life** that you might otherwise avoid, fear, or try to change. It teaches you to stop fighting against your environment and instead cultivate an attitude of acceptance, growth, and presence.

This practice isn't about denying discomfort or pretending that everything is perfect. It's about choosing to be at peace with the present moment, even when it's difficult. It encourages you to **shift your mindset from judgment to**

acceptance, transforming difficult situations into stepping stones for personal development.

Whether you're facing a challenging work environment, dealing with past emotional pain, or simply struggling to relax in your bedroom at night, the Perfect Space Activity offers a tool for **finding peace wherever you are**. It empowers you to realize that no space—no matter how challenging—is beyond the reach of your growth, healing, and peace.

In time, this practice can help you develop a deeper sense of **self-mastery**. You will become more resilient in the face of adversity, more present in your daily life, and more capable of finding peace in any situation. Remember, everything, in its own time, is perfect now.

The **Perfect Space Activity** isn't just a method for dealing with discomfort; it's a mindset shift that can deeply transform the way you experience the world. By reducing resistance, fostering emotional growth, enhancing your presence, and reducing stress, it helps you face life with greater resilience and acceptance. With regular practice, you will find yourself navigating challenging spaces with a sense of calm and empowerment, knowing that every space you encounter holds potential for learning and growth.

Activity 4: How to Fall in Love with Life Again

The Front Door Activity: A Simple Practice for Profound Change

The **Front Door Activity** is a deceptively simple practice that can have a profound impact on how you experience your daily life. By focusing on cultivating positive emotions like **excitement**, **gratitude**, and **compassion** during key moments of your day—specifically when you leave and return home—you create an energetic shift that can transform your emotional state and improve your overall mindset.

Before we begin, I'd like you to keep in mind: The Front Door Activity Does Not Make You 'Soft'... It Makes You Happier, More Efficient, Productive, and Results-Oriented

Phase 1

This initial phase consists of two main Steps:

Leaving Your Home

When you leave your home for the day, the Front Door Activity encourages you to set an intention for how you want to feel as you enter the outside world. This is an opportunity to leave behind any stress or negativity from your home environment and approach the day with fresh energy. Before stepping out, take a moment to:

- **Pause and Breathe**: Stand still for a few seconds before leaving. Take a deep breath, clear your mind, and let go of any lingering stress.
- **Set an Emotional Intention**: Choose a positive emotion to anchor yourself in for the day. This might be **excitement** about the day ahead, **gratitude** for the opportunities that await, or **compassion** towards yourself and others.
- **Visualize a Positive Transition**: As you imagine stepping out, envision a smooth and joyful transition from your home environment to the outside world, creating a mental space that aligns with your chosen emotion.

By consciously cultivating positive emotions at this point, you set the tone for the rest of your day. You leave your home with intention, rather than just reacting to external circumstances.

Returning Home

When you return home, the Front Door Activity helps you shift from your external world—whether it was stressful or fulfilling—back to your sanctuary. As you re-enter, it's easy to carry the weight of your day's challenges with you.

The practice encourages you to pause at the front door, letting go of any outside tension before you enter. Here's how to do it:

- **Pause at the Front Door**: Before entering your home, take a moment to physically stop at the threshold. Breathe deeply and release any external stress or negativity you may have carried with you.
- **Shift Your Energy**: As you stand there, imagine leaving behind anything you don't want to bring into your home. Picture the outside world being left on the other side of the door.
- **Set a Positive Intention for Your Homecoming**: Choose an emotion that you want to bring into your home—peace, joy, love, or connection. Visualize how this energy will affect your interactions and the atmosphere in your space.
- **Express Gratitude**: As you step inside, take a moment to express gratitude for your home and the people within it. Cultivating this sense of appreciation can transform your emotional state and help you fully embrace the sanctuary of your home.

This phase of the Front Door Activity ensures that you re-enter your home with a clean emotional slate, free from the stress of the outside world. It fosters a sense of presence and balance as you reconnect with your loved ones and your space.

The Front Door Activity works by anchoring **positive emotions** at the key transitions of your day. Emotional anchoring is a technique that helps you create specific associations between emotions and physical locations or actions. When you repeatedly practice this ritual, your brain begins to link these emotions with the act of leaving and returning home, making it easier to shift your mindset and energy in a positive direction.

1. **Creating Emotional Resilience**: By actively practicing emotional shifts when transitioning between spaces, you build resilience to external stressors. You become more capable of choosing how you respond to life's challenges instead of simply reacting.
2. **Building Positive Energy**: By focusing on gratitude, compassion,

and positive intention, you create a ripple effect of positive energy that extends throughout your day and home environment.

3. **Reinforcing Positive Habits**: This small ritual reinforces the habit of emotional awareness and emotional regulation. You consciously choose to set the tone for your day and your home environment, which can lead to greater overall emotional balance.

Key Takeaways:

- **Two Phases**: The Front Door Activity consists of two main rituals: one for leaving home with positive intention, and one for returning home with a reset emotional state.
- **Cultivate Positive Emotions**: Each phase encourages you to anchor emotions like excitement, gratitude, and compassion at pivotal moments of your day.
- **Emotional Transition**: By using the front door as a symbolic threshold, you shift your energy from the outside world to your internal world, fostering emotional balance and peace.
- **Simple but Transformative**: While the practice is small, it has the potential to deeply shift how you experience daily life by consciously choosing emotional states at the start and end of your day.

Incorporating the Front Door Activity into your daily routine helps you start and end your day with intention, creating a powerful emotional shift that improves your mindset, enhances your energy, and deepens your connection with yourself and others.

Let me repeat:

Step 1: Cultivating Excitement and Adventure

The first part of the **Front Door Activity** is about setting a positive tone as you step out into the world. Rather than leaving your home as a routine task or obligation, this step invites you to infuse your departure with feelings of **excitement, curiosity**, and **adventure**. By consciously shifting your mindset, you can transform even the most ordinary moments into opportunities for growth and exploration.

Walking Out the Front Door: Infusing Excitement and Adventure

When you leave your home, pause for a moment to connect with a feeling of **excitement**. Visualize the world outside as full of new possibilities, ready for you to explore. Whether your day feels predictable or filled with obligations, mentally prepare yourself to stay open to the unexpected.

- **Focus on Possibility**: Imagine that stepping out the door is the beginning of an exciting journey, even if it's just another workday or errand. Visualize this step as one toward **discovery**, **learning**, and **connection**.

- **Cultivate Curiosity**: Ask yourself questions like, "What amazing thing might happen today?" or "What new opportunities are waiting for me?" Allow these questions to spark a sense of adventure in your mind.

- **Set the Tone for the Day**: For just a few moments, feel the energy of **adventure** and **open-mindedness**. Let go of any thoughts of the past or future and focus on being present with the excitement of what today might bring.

This intentional shift primes your **brain** to view the world as a place of **opportunity** rather than obligation. By approaching each day with a sense of **excitement**, you train yourself to remain **open** and **receptive** to new experiences. Even if your day is predictable or routine, adopting an adventurous mindset helps you see **possibilities** instead of simply completing tasks. Over time, this perspective becomes a habit, making even the most mundane activities feel exciting and filled with potential.

Example:

Imagine you're heading out for a workday. Normally, you'd feel the familiar blend of **routine** and **stress**. But before you leave the house, you pause. Instead of thinking of the day as just another workday, you remind yourself that it's an opportunity to learn something new, meet interesting people, or solve a challenging problem in a creative way. As you step out the door, you feel a **surge of excitement**, knowing that today holds something **fresh** and **exciting**—whether it's an unexpected encounter or a breakthrough idea. This shift in mindset helps you approach your work with more energy, **enthusiasm**, and **curiosity**.

Remember

- Stepping out with **intention** transforms your departure from home into a powerful emotional reset.
- Focusing on **excitement** and **adventure** shifts your mindset, making you more open to new experiences and opportunities.
- This practice helps you break free from routine and approach even the most predictable days with **curiosity** and **positivity**.
- Over time, this mindset becomes habitual, helping you navigate your life with **more enthusiasm** and a deeper sense of **purpose**.

By cultivating excitement and adventure at the front door, you create a ripple effect that influences the entire day, making each moment feel alive with potential.

OUT THE FRONT DOOR = ADVENTURE AND EXCITEMENT

Got it!

Step 2: Walking In the Front Door: Gratitude and Compassion

The second part of the **Front Door Activity** focuses on how you re-enter your home at the end of the day. After being out in the world, it's easy to return home feeling **exhausted, frustrated,** or **disconnected**. However, by taking a moment to pause as you walk in, you can **transform** the way you reconnect with your space and the people inside it, shifting from weariness to **gratitude** and **compassion**.

Walking In the Door: Cultivating Gratitude and Compassion

When you come home, take a few seconds to stop at the door and bring your attention to the present moment. This intentional pause can create an emotional shift that helps you ground yourself before fully entering your home.

- **Focus on Gratitude:**
  As you stand at the threshold, take in your surroundings. Feel

thankful for the simple, often-overlooked blessings—such as having a roof over your head, warmth, food, safety, or a familiar space. Gratitude moves your attention from what may be missing to what is already **present** in your life, cultivating a sense of abundance and contentment.

- Reflect on the things that may go unnoticed in the hustle of daily life, like a comfortable chair, the warmth of your home, or a place to relax.
- Shift your mindset from scarcity to **abundance**, embracing the peace and comfort of your home.

- **Cultivate Compassion:**
  Once you've grounded yourself in **gratitude**, turn your focus to the people inside your home—whether it's family, roommates, or even yourself. Take a moment to feel **compassion** for everyone you encounter. Recognize that, just like you, they have their own set of challenges and emotions, and that everyone is doing the best they can in their own way.

  - Acknowledge their struggles and victories, and remind yourself to approach them with **empathy**.
  - Practice understanding, knowing that both joy and sorrow are universal experiences that bind us all.

By combining gratitude for your surroundings with compassion for the people in your life, you create a **positive emotional environment** that can neutralize the stress and strain from the outside world. This practice fosters a sense of emotional balance, making it easier to interact with others in a **kind**, **grounded**, and **present** way.

Why This Works:

- **Gratitude** shifts your focus away from what's missing or what you lack, and brings attention to the abundance and blessings already in your life. This creates emotional stability and reduces feelings of discontent or exhaustion.
- **Compassion** fosters **deeper connections** and understanding, helping

you approach your loved ones or housemates with more **kindness**, empathy, and patience. It reminds you that everyone has their own emotional landscape, which promotes a peaceful, harmonious home environment.

- By practicing these emotions at the **entrance** to your home, you can reframe your experience of coming back, turning what could be a moment of fatigue or stress into a **rejuvenating**, emotionally nourishing transition.

Example:

Imagine you've had a long, stressful day at work. You're tired, and you just want to **unwind**. But before entering your home, you pause. You take a deep breath and shift your perspective. You feel **grateful** for having a safe and comfortable space to return to—something that many people in the world don't have. You take a moment to **appreciate** the home you've worked hard to create.

Then, as you step inside, you remind yourself that your loved ones may have had their own difficulties that day. They might be dealing with challenges you don't know about. You approach them with **compassion**, understanding that everyone has their own emotional load to carry. This mindset helps you stay **present** and respond **gently** to those around you, creating a **calm, peaceful** atmosphere as you reconnect with your home life.

Key Takeaways:

- **Gratitude** helps you focus on the blessings you have, shifting your energy from lack to abundance.
- **Compassion** helps you connect with others on a deeper level, recognizing that everyone has their own emotional experiences.
- This practice creates a **calm, peaceful environment** in your home, helping you to be more present and engaged with the people around you.
- Pausing before entering your home allows you to **reset emotionally**, creating a sense of balance and emotional well-being before interacting with your loved ones.

By practicing **gratitude** and **compassion** as you walk in the door, you reframe your return home as a moment of emotional **rejuvenation**, fostering a sense of **peace** and **connection** with your space and the people you share it with.

OUT THE FRONT DOOR = ADVENTURE AND EXCITEMENT

IN THE FRONT DOOR = ADVENTURE AND EXCITEMENT

Got it? Now go practice it.

Now!

Why the Front Door Activity Works

The **Front Door Activity** is a simple yet powerful practice that can dramatically shift your emotional and mental state. It works by leveraging the transformative power of **ritual** and **intention** at two key transitions during your day—leaving and returning home. These brief moments, while small, provide emotional "bookends" that set the tone for your mindset and energy throughout the day. Here's why this practice is so effective:

Shifts Focus from Routine to Experience

- The **Front Door Activity** helps break the habit of viewing daily routines as mundane or automatic tasks. Instead of simply rushing out the door or back into your home, you train yourself to **engage with each transition mindfully**, focusing on the potential for positive experiences in the moment.

- By infusing these moments with **intention**, you train your brain to see every part of your day—whether exciting or routine—as an opportunity for growth, positivity, and emotional engagement. This shift can bring a greater sense of **joy** and **fulfillment** to even the most repetitive tasks, turning ordinary moments into a chance to feel present and energized.

Builds Emotional Resilience

- The practice encourages you to **acknowledge** your emotional state when you leave and return home. This act of emotional awareness helps you stay grounded, which makes it easier to handle stress, challenges, or unexpected events throughout your day.
- By consistently choosing to ground yourself in **positive emotions** (such as excitement when leaving and gratitude or compassion when returning), you build emotional **resilience**. Over time, this allows you to respond to difficult situations with more awareness and balance rather than reacting impulsively or emotionally.

Fosters Connection and Kindness

- The emphasis on **gratitude** and **compassion**—especially as you re-enter your home—cultivates a sense of emotional **connection** with both yourself and others. Focusing on these positive emotions when you step through your front door fosters a **culture of kindness**, empathy, and understanding within your household.
- This practice doesn't just improve your relationship with those around you; it also nurtures a sense of **self-compassion**. It's a reminder that you, too, deserve kindness and understanding, helping to create a more supportive and harmonious environment at home.

Key Benefits of the Front Door Activity:

- **Shifts Perspective**: Transforms everyday routines into opportunities for joy, curiosity, and positivity.
- **Emotional Grounding**: Helps you process and address emotions intentionally, making you more resilient in the face of daily challenges.
- **Enhanced Relationships**: Promotes gratitude and compassion, leading to stronger connections with others and creating a more peaceful home environment.

Consistent Practice, Profound Results

The **Front Door Activity** may only take a few seconds each day, but it has the power to significantly impact your emotional and mental state. By cultivating **positive emotions** at key moments—before leaving and after returning home—you lay the foundation for a more peaceful, connected, and emotionally balanced life. Over time, these brief moments of reflection become a **habit** that enhances your ability to approach life with **joy**, **resilience**, and **clarity**.

With consistent practice, the **Front Door Activity** can bring greater **peace**, **connection**, and **happiness** to your daily experience, creating a life that feels more open, intentional, and full of possibility.

Have you practiced yet?

Go do it!

Focus on Phase 1 today. All day! No rush.

Phase 2

Expanding the Practice to Any Front Door You Walk Through

In Phase 1, we focused on shifting your emotional energy when leaving and entering your home. In Phase 2, we now broaden this practice to include *any* front door you walk through, whether it's your office, a store, a meeting, or a social gathering. Each doorway becomes an opportunity for positive transformation, helping you create new habits of emotional presence, gratitude, and excitement.

The goal is to integrate this practice into your daily life, cultivating a mindset of openness and emotional balance wherever you go.

Walking In Any Front Door: Gratitude and Compassion

When you enter any space—whether it's your office, a café, or a friend's house—take a moment to ground yourself in gratitude and compassion. This helps you connect more deeply with the present moment and with the people you encounter. These small pauses can significantly enhance your emotional state and interactions throughout the day.

Gratitude

Pause for a second and take a deep breath as you enter. Acknowledge the simple fact that you're able to be there. Whether you're entering a store, a meeting, or a friend's home, express gratitude for the opportunity to be in this space, to connect with others, or to experience something new. Even if the visit is brief, appreciating the moment shifts your mindset to one of abundance rather than taking things for granted.

Compassion

After grounding yourself in gratitude, allow compassion to fill you. Recognize that everyone you encounter—whether it's the cashier, a colleague, or a stranger—is going through their own unique experience. Send them a silent thought of kindness and understanding. Whether the interaction is short or long, this act of compassion fosters a sense of connection and makes your encounters more meaningful.

Example: Café Encounter You walk into a busy café to meet a friend. Instead of rushing, you pause at the door. Feel gratitude for the opportunity to connect with your friend. As you order coffee, silently offer compassion to the barista, acknowledging that they, too, are going through their own life experiences. By the time you sit down, you've set the tone for a more connected, compassionate interaction with everyone around you.

Example: Entering Your Car As you enter your car, take a moment to feel gratitude. Appreciate that you have a car, that it's in working condition, and that it has enough fuel to get you where you need to go. Whether it's a short drive or a long journey, this simple act of gratitude shifts your mindset from routine to appreciation for what you have.

Then, as you start the engine, extend compassion to anyone else in the car with you, and even to other drivers on the road. Acknowledge that every person on the road is facing their own challenges and struggles. If everyone practiced this mindset—pausing to feel gratitude and compassion—there would be no road rage, only understanding and calm. This simple shift creates a peaceful, more mindful driving experience.

By practicing gratitude and compassion regularly, you turn even mundane moments into opportunities for emotional grounding and connection, enriching both your inner life and your interactions with others.

Walking Out Any Front Door: Excitement and Adventure

When leaving any place—whether home, work, or elsewhere—continue applying the excitement and adventure mindset from Step 1. See every transition as an opportunity for growth, connection, or discovery.

How to Apply This: Before you leave any space, take a deep breath and think, "I'm entering something new." Even if it's routine, visualize the space as filled with potential. This primes your mind to be open and receptive to whatever unfolds, no matter how small or big.

Example: Heading to work? Instead of just going through the motions, pause at the door and think, "Today holds new possibilities. I might meet interesting people, face exciting challenges, or learn something valuable." Walk through that door with the energy of possibility, even on the busiest days.

Leaving the Door: Excitement and Adventure

As you leave any space—whether it's your office, a store, a friend's home, or even your car—return to the energy of excitement and adventure. This is your moment to reset, shifting from the completion of one experience to the anticipation of the next. Embrace each transition as an opportunity for something new, inspiring, or enriching.

How to Apply This

Before you step out of any location, take a moment to pause, breathe deeply, and consciously think, **"What's next? What new opportunities await?"** Whether you're finishing a meeting, wrapping up an errand, or leaving your car, approach the next step with the curiosity and excitement of discovering something new. This shift in mindset helps you view each transition not as a routine, but as an opening for new possibilities.

Example: Leaving a Work Meeting

You've just finished a meeting at work and feel drained. Instead of focusing on the exhaustion or any lingering frustrations, take a deep breath before exiting the room. Tell yourself, **"I'm stepping into the next opportunity."** Whether it's meeting a friend, running an errand, or getting started on a new project, reset your energy and approach the next transition with excitement, knowing it could bring something fresh.

Example: Exiting Your Car

As you step out of your car, take a moment to pause and feel a sense of adventure. Before heading into your home, office, or any new location, mentally frame the moment as a chance to embrace what comes next. Think of this next step as a gateway to something positive. Perhaps you're about to meet someone, run an errand, or just enjoy the next part of your day. By taking a breath and focusing on the excitement of what's to come, you turn the transition of leaving your car into an opportunity for new experiences.

By practicing this shift, you reframe every exit as a door to something new. Whether leaving your car, office, or any space, you cultivate a mindset of excitement and curiosity, welcoming each next step with a sense of adventure.

Why This Expanded Practice Works

Expanding the **Front Door Activity** to include all doors (in particular front doors) you walk through—whether at home, work, in your car, or in public spaces—gives you a powerful tool for emotional reset throughout your day. Each door becomes a symbolic transition, helping you shift your emotional energy and move through life with more presence, adaptability, and empathy. Here's why this expanded practice is so effective:

Greater Emotional Flexibility

By consciously shifting your emotional energy as you pass through different doors, you practice **emotional flexibility**. Each time you enter or exit a space with intention—whether it's excitement, gratitude, or compassion—you're training yourself to **take charge of your emotions** rather than allowing them to be dictated by external factors. This shift from reactive to proactive emotional management builds resilience, helping you approach challenges with greater calm and awareness.

More Connection with Others

Integrating **compassion** into every transition strengthens your **connection with others**. By recognizing the shared humanity of everyone you encounter—whether it's a colleague, a stranger, or a friend—you foster a deeper sense of empathy and understanding. This awareness enhances your interpersonal relationships, creating a **more harmonious, compassionate environment** wherever you go. It's a small act that helps build emotional intimacy and a sense of peace, knowing you've treated others with kindness.

Reframing Routine to Ritual

This practice allows you to **reframe routine actions** into meaningful rituals. Rather than passively going through the motions of entering and exiting spaces, you transform each door into an opportunity to reset your emotional energy. Whether you're entering a meeting, exiting your car, or walking into your home, each moment becomes a **ritual of mindfulness** that breaks the monotony of daily life. By choosing to approach each transition with excitement, gratitude, or compassion, you make the ordinary extraordinary and fill your day with **purpose and emotional empowerment**.

The **Expanded Front Door Activity** is a deceptively simple practice with powerful benefits. By shifting your emotional state at key moments throughout your day, you cultivate a mindset of **adventure, gratitude, and compassion**, turning every doorway into a gateway to new possibilities. This habit not only enhances your **emotional resilience** but also makes your interactions with others more positive and meaningful. Over time, this practice transforms your perspective on life, helping you approach the world with more openness, balance, and positivity. Through consistent application, this simple practice can profoundly **enhance the way you experience daily life**.

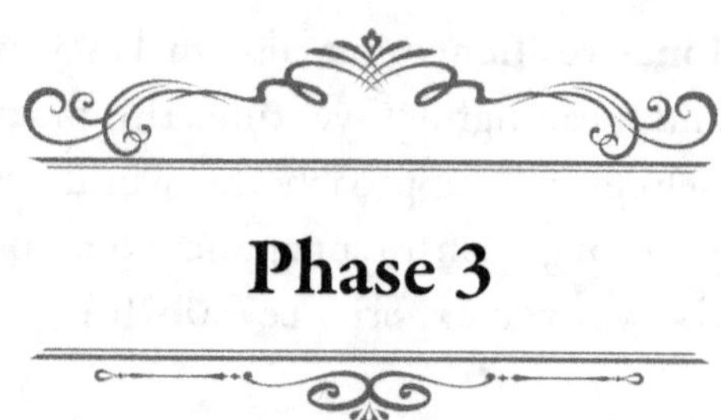

Phase 3

Sending Energy to Those Around You

In **Phase 3** of the Front Door Activity, we take the practice a step further by extending our emotional energy outward, focusing on **sending positive energy** to those around us. This shift moves from personal emotional alignment to actively influencing the energy of others. By consciously sending positive vibrations—like **gratitude**, **compassion**, **excitement**, and **adventure**—you can transform not only your interactions but the overall energy of your environment.

This Phase empowers you to actively influence your surroundings, shaping your relationships and the tone of your day with the emotional goals you want to cultivate. Over time, sending positive energy will create a **ripple effect**, impacting how people feel around you and how they respond to you, fostering a more positive, connected, and harmonious atmosphere.

When Someone Walks Toward You: Gratitude and Compassion

As people approach you, when they *enter* your space—whether they're colleagues, strangers, or loved ones—you have a powerful opportunity to **send gratitude and compassion** their way. You may not know their personal challenges, but in these moments, you can acknowledge them as fellow human beings, navigating their own journey. By sending them positive energy, you enhance the interaction and foster goodwill.

How to Apply This:

- **Pause and Acknowledge:** When someone walks toward you, take a moment to stop and notice their presence. Instead of rushing by, focus your energy on them.
- **Send Gratitude and Compassion:** Without expecting anything in

return, silently express gratitude and compassion. Think, "I'm grateful for this person's presence, and I wish them kindness and understanding on their journey."

- **Visualize Positive Energy**: Picture a **warm, golden light** radiating from you, enveloping the person as they approach. This visual helps to invite positivity and connection into the moment, influencing the energy of the interaction.

Example:

You're walking through a busy office and cross paths with a colleague you don't interact with much. Instead of just walking past, you pause for a moment. In that split second, you silently send them gratitude for their contributions and compassion for any challenges they may be facing. You don't need to say anything aloud—just your energy shifts. The next time you interact with this colleague, they may respond with more warmth, openness, or appreciation, subtly strengthening your connection.

By consciously sending positive energy to those around you, you amplify your emotional goals and foster a **greater sense of unity**. This practice cultivates an environment where people feel seen, appreciated, and understood, making it easier to build meaningful relationships and create positive interactions, whether at work, at home, or in any other environment.

Why This Works

Sending positive energy—particularly gratitude and compassion—toward others works because it engages your emotional and energetic state on a deeper, more meaningful level. While you may not know the personal struggles or joys of those around you, by consciously acknowledging their humanity, you **create a bond** that transcends surface-level interactions. You recognize that everyone has their own journey, and in doing so, you open the door to more authentic, positive exchanges.

Here's why this works:

- **Acknowledging Shared Humanity**: When you send gratitude and compassion, you acknowledge the other person as a fellow human being with their own life, challenges, and experiences. This small but powerful shift creates an emotional connection that goes beyond the usual transactional nature of most interactions.

- **Fostering Reciprocity**: People are naturally drawn to those who radiate **kindness** and **understanding**. By putting positive energy out into the world, you invite it to come back to you. Over time, others are more likely to mirror your energy, reciprocating with warmth, openness, and positivity.

- **Creating a Peaceful, Nonjudgmental Space**: By sending out feelings of compassion and gratitude, you contribute to a **peaceful and accepting atmosphere**. You foster an environment where people feel safe to be themselves without judgment. This promotes better communication, less conflict, and more harmonious interactions.

- **Enhancing Relationships**: Whether in professional or personal settings, sending positive energy helps build rapport, trust, and goodwill. It can make even brief encounters feel more meaningful, and it creates a foundation for stronger, more supportive relationships over time.

Ultimately, this practice enhances your emotional **resilience** and **empathy**, not just for the people around you but also for yourself. You start to radiate a sense of **peace**, and this attracts more positive energy back to you. The more you practice sending gratitude, compassion, and understanding, the more your relationships—both personal and professional—will flourish, transforming your interactions into moments of connection and growth.

When Someone Walks Away: Excitement and Adventure

When someone walks away from you, when they *exit* your space—whether they're leaving a conversation, exiting a meeting, or simply moving on to the next part of their day—you have an opportunity to consciously shift your energy into **excitement** and **adventure**. Instead of feeling a sense of loss or ending, you can embrace the feeling that life is always unfolding with new opportunities, even as people move on.

How to Apply This:

- **Stay emotionally engaged as they leave**, but shift your focus to excitement. Rather than mourning the end of an interaction, reframe it as a part of the flow of life and the potential for what comes next.

- **Visualize their path as full of possibilities.** As the person walks away, mentally wish them well on whatever their next step may be. Imagine their life unfolding with new adventures, and allow that to energize you as well.
- **Embrace the excitement of what's next** for you. Even if it's just a small task or the next meeting, cultivate a sense of anticipation and curiosity about what's coming. This helps you stay emotionally open and engaged with life, making every moment feel like part of an exciting journey.

Example:

Imagine you're in a meeting, and a colleague shares their thoughts. Once they finish speaking and the conversation winds down, instead of feeling like it's the end of something, you shift your mindset. You think, "What will they do next? I'm excited to see what they accomplish." As they walk away, you feel anticipation for your next task or conversation. You embrace the idea that the day will continue unfolding with exciting opportunities, whether it's another meeting, a personal moment, or a creative endeavor.

Why This Works:

By shifting your energy from a feeling of **loss** to one of **possibility** and **excitement**, you maintain a high-vibration energy that keeps you open to life's next chapter, no matter how small it seems. The energy you send out when someone leaves you—whether physically or emotionally—affects your perception of that departure. Instead of feeling sad or disappointed, you create an emotional space where every moment feels like a transition into something new and meaningful.

This mindset helps you stay grounded in **anticipation** rather than **regret**. It reinforces the idea that no interaction or experience is ever truly over. Even when someone leaves your presence, the flow of life continues, and the next phase is just as exciting as the last. By embracing this, you train yourself to live in a state of **constant discovery**, where every moment is an opportunity for growth and adventure.

Why This Phase Is Powerful: Sending Energy to Those Around You

Phase 3 of the Front Door Activity—**Sending Energy to Those Around You**—is grounded in the understanding that our emotions are contagious. Our energy has the power to not only influence our own mental and emotional state but also to shape the energy of those we interact with. By consciously sending gratitude, compassion, excitement, and adventure to others, you create a positive emotional environment that can uplift and influence everyone around you.

Cultivating a Positive Emotional Ecosystem

When you radiate positive energy, you help to foster a supportive, harmonious environment wherever you go. Whether you're at work, social events, or just running errands, the energy you project has a ripple effect. People are naturally drawn to kindness and warmth. As you send out gratitude and compassion, you attract more of the same back, making your interactions more pleasant and fulfilling. By consistently practicing this, you create an ecosystem where positivity thrives, which increases your chances of good collaboration, communication, and connection.

Strengthening Your Emotional Influence

Every time you consciously send gratitude, compassion, or excitement to someone, you exercise emotional influence. You can't control others' feelings, but you can guide the emotional current of an interaction by offering positive energy. This enhances your ability to remain emotionally present and resilient, no matter what's going on around you. Over time, this strengthens your emotional influence, making you someone who not only understands others but also creates an environment where others feel safe, supported, and valued.

Strengthening Relationships

Sending gratitude and compassion to people as they walk toward you nurtures deeper, more meaningful relationships. People are more likely to feel emotionally connected to you when they sense your genuine acknowledgment of their humanity. Whether it's a colleague, friend, or stranger, a small act of sending positive energy can create bonds that go beyond superficial interactions. Similarly, when you send excitement and adventure as someone walks away, you reinforce the emotional connection without feeling the loss of the interaction. Instead, you stay open to the next moment and feel energized by the continuous flow of opportunities life brings.

A Ripple Effect of Positivity

Phase 3 of the Front Door Activity is a powerful extension of the practice that turns emotional energy into a tool for positive transformation. By consciously sending energy in the form of **gratitude, compassion, excitement,** and **adventure**—whether to someone approaching you or leaving you—you elevate the emotional tone of every space you enter. You contribute to creating an atmosphere of connection, empathy, and shared human experience, where every encounter becomes an opportunity to share positivity and grow together.

This practice reinforces a simple yet profound truth: **we are all interconnected.** Not only do we affect our own emotional state, but we can also uplift those around us, sending out ripples of positivity that create a more supportive, fulfilling world. Whether it's at work, at home, or in social settings, when we choose to consciously send positive energy, we set the stage for richer, more rewarding interactions, and contribute to creating a collective emotional atmosphere that supports growth and connection.

Phase 4

Embracing Love and Peace

In Phase 4 of the Front Door Activity, the emotional shifts you've been practicing—**excitement**, **adventure**, **gratitude**, and **compassion**—become second nature in your day-to-day life. Now that these positive emotions are flowing with ease, it's time to deepen your emotional practice and introduce two of the most powerful, transformative forces: **love** and **peace**.

These emotions transcend simple positivity. They are universal forces that can **heal**, **unite**, and create **profound connections** between people. When you consciously send love and peace to others, you don't just elevate your emotional state—you contribute to the harmony of your environment and the world around you.

Sending Love and Peace to Others

In Phase 4, you'll learn to extend the positive energy you've been cultivating to the people around you—whether in person or in your thoughts. **Love** and **peace** radiate deeply calming and harmonious energy, transforming not just your interactions but also the emotional landscape of the spaces you enter.

How to Apply This:

As You Meet People

Whether it's a close friend, a colleague, a family member, or even a stranger, take a moment to silently wish them **love** and **peace**. This doesn't require words, only intention. It's about radiating positive energy without expecting anything in return, simply wishing them well from a place of genuine care and connection.

- **Example**: As you walk past a colleague in the hallway, take a second to silently say, "I wish you love and peace on your path." You don't need to speak it out loud or draw attention to it; simply let the energy of that thought fill the space between you. It creates an unspoken bond that can subtly shift the emotional atmosphere in your interactions.

In Your Thoughts

You can also extend love and peace toward people in your life—even those you aren't directly interacting with. Think of someone who may be going through a tough time, such as a friend, a family member, or even someone in the news. Send them healing thoughts of love and peace, visualizing them surrounded by a soft, calming light, and focusing your intention on their well-being.

- **Example**: Imagine a friend who is struggling with a personal challenge. You can take a moment to mentally picture them bathed in a warm, peaceful light, sending them silent thoughts of encouragement and support. This simple act can create a profound emotional shift for both you and them, even if they don't directly know about it.

Maintain a Peaceful Energy

When entering environments that could be tense or challenging—whether it's a busy meeting, a stressful situation, or even just a crowded space—**intentionally bring peace with you**. Focus on maintaining a sense of calm, and carry that peaceful energy into the room, influencing the atmosphere and everyone within it.

- **Example**: You walk into a bustling coffee shop, and the environment feels chaotic—people are rushing, the line is long, and the noise is high. Instead of getting caught up in the rush, pause for a moment. Close your eyes for a beat and send silent love and peace to everyone in the space. Visualize them enjoying their moment in line, relaxed, and at ease. This subtle shift in energy helps to defuse tension and brings calm to the environment.

Why This Works:

By sending **love** and **peace** to others, you're not only creating a positive environment for them, but you're also reinforcing your own inner peace. These emotions, when practiced consistently, not only shift the energy of any given space but also cultivate a deeper sense of connection and compassion with the world around you. This practice helps you move through the world more gracefully, regardless of external circumstances, and can positively influence everything from interactions with strangers to close relationships. By embracing love and peace, you transform not only the moment but also your experience of life.

Remember: Sending Love and Peace, It's About Raising Your Energy

Here are several more examples of how you can apply **love** and **peace** in different environments, in line with the spirit of Phase 4 in the Front Door Activity:

Walking Through a Shopping Center:

You're walking through a busy shopping center, and the crowds are thick. People are rushing, checking their phones, some appearing stressed. Instead of matching the pace or getting irritated by the crowds, pause for a second. Take a deep breath, and with your next exhale, mentally send peace to those around you. Picture them feeling at ease, moving through their day with calm energy. You can silently say to yourself, "I wish peace and ease to everyone I pass." This simple act helps create a soothing ripple effect in an otherwise hectic environment, calming both you and others.

Example: As you pass a mother pushing a stroller, her arms full and her face showing signs of exhaustion, you silently send love and peace her way. Visualize her finding a moment of relief, feeling supported, and knowing she's doing an incredible job. You might even feel a slight shift in your own energy as you realize that kindness doesn't need to be spoken to be felt.

At Work in a Meeting:

You're sitting in a meeting at work. The energy feels a little tense—perhaps a colleague is frustrated, or there's a disagreement on the table. Instead of adding to the tension or feeling uncomfortable, pause for a moment. Take a deep breath, silently sending peace to everyone in the room. Visualize the group coming to a calm, mutual understanding, and everyone leaving the room with clarity and unity. You can also send love to each participant, wishing them a peaceful resolution to the conversation, no matter what the outcome is.

Example: During the meeting, a team member expresses their disagreement in a way that feels charged. Instead of feeling defensive or stressed, take a deep breath, and send them love. Visualize them feeling heard, understood, and at ease with their perspective. Then, imagine peace settling over the entire room, allowing for a more productive and respectful conversation moving forward.

At a Party or Social Gathering:

You walk into a lively party or social gathering, where people are mingling and conversations are happening all around you. You might feel overwhelmed by the noise or unsure of where to fit in. Instead of becoming anxious, pause for a moment, take a deep breath, and silently send love and peace to everyone in the room. Visualize the space as one of warm, welcoming energy, where everyone feels seen, heard, and valued.

Example: A friend is telling an animated story, and a few people seem distracted or not fully engaged. You silently send peace to everyone in the group, imagining the conversation flowing smoothly and everyone feeling heard. As you do this, you might notice a sense of calm within yourself, and the interactions around you may feel more grounded and connected.

At Home:

You've had a long day, and you're finally home. The house feels a bit chaotic—perhaps there are things to clean up or people in your home who are stressed or in their own emotional spaces. Rather than letting any of that energy affect you, take a deep breath as you walk in the door. Silently send love and peace to the people you live with, wishing them well and hoping they feel at ease. Visualize the space being filled with warmth and harmony.

Example: Your partner is on the phone, seeming agitated. Instead of letting their stress affect you, pause. Send a silent wish of peace for their moment, imagining them transitioning into a more peaceful state. You might also send love to yourself, grounding in the knowledge that you're home now, and you can create a peaceful environment.

In Public Transit or Traffic:

You're sitting on a crowded bus or in traffic, surrounded by people who might be rushing, frustrated, or stressed. Rather than getting caught in the collective tension, take a moment to shift your energy. Send love and peace to the people around you. Visualize them arriving at their destinations feeling calm and at ease.

Example: You're stuck in traffic, and the cars around you are moving slowly. You notice a driver in a hurry, visibly agitated. Instead of letting their frustration affect you, silently send them peace. Visualize them taking a deep breath, letting go of the tension, and driving with ease. This mental shift can help you feel more relaxed in your own car, too.

In a Doctor's Office or Waiting Room:

You're sitting in a doctor's office or waiting room, where everyone is likely feeling some form of anxiety, whether it's about the upcoming appointment or concerns about their health. Instead of feeling tense or overwhelmed by the collective worry, pause for a moment and silently send love and peace to everyone in the room. Visualize the entire space being filled with calm energy, where everyone feels reassured and at ease.

Example: A patient across from you is nervously tapping their foot. You silently send them love, imagining them receiving healing energy and feeling at peace with whatever is ahead of them. This energy can uplift not only the other person but also help to ease your own anxiety as well.

Walking Into a School or Educational Setting:

You enter a classroom, a school hallway, or an educational seminar. The energy may feel intense, whether it's the pressure of an upcoming test or the hustle and bustle of people trying to get to their next class. Instead of feeling stressed by the environment, you take a moment to breathe deeply and send peace and love to the students, teachers, and staff. Visualize a calming atmosphere that allows everyone to feel supported in their learning.

Example: A student seems visibly stressed, perhaps before an important presentation. As you walk past, you silently wish them peace and calm, imagining them standing tall and speaking confidently. By holding this intention, you contribute to a more supportive atmosphere for both them and yourself.

Why This Works:

Sending **love** and **peace** to others is a powerful way to elevate your emotional frequency and spread positive energy throughout your interactions. These emotions, especially when practiced intentionally, create an atmosphere of safety, connection, and warmth. Love and peace are universal emotional currencies—they can break down barriers, dissolve conflict, and foster deeper connections between people, regardless of their circumstances.

By **quietly wishing others love and peace**, you create an invisible but potent bond that transcends words and actions. It's a way of honoring the shared humanity between you and others, contributing to a greater sense of unity and understanding. Whether through direct interaction or simply holding these intentions, you're becoming an active participant in creating a world that feels more compassionate, harmonious, and connected.

Example of the Ripple Effect:

- **In Your Environment**: Imagine walking into a meeting where the energy feels heavy or tense. By consciously bringing peace with you and visualizing love flowing into the space, you shift the emotional tone of the room. This calmness can spread to others, subtly influencing the atmosphere and encouraging more cooperative and respectful dialogue.
- **In Your Daily Life**: On your way home from work, you might encounter a stressful moment in traffic or in the store. Instead of getting frustrated, take a deep breath and send out thoughts of peace to everyone around you, including other drivers, fellow shoppers, or workers. By practicing this, you're actively choosing not to engage in negative emotions but to redirect that energy toward love and peace, helping to mitigate stress and maintain your inner balance.

Embracing Love and Peace:

In Phase 4, you take the energy you've cultivated in earlier stages of the Front Door Activity and elevate it to a more expansive level. Love and peace are transformative forces, not only within you but within the world around you. By consciously sending love and peace, you not only uplift yourself but also create a wave of positive energy that touches everyone you encounter.

Sending Love and Peace: Remember, It's About You

In Phase 4 of the Front Door Activity, you're not just shifting your energy for others—sending **love** and **peace** is primarily about YOU. These powerful emotions help you **elevate your own emotional state**, creating harmony within yourself and in your surroundings. When you consciously choose to send love and peace to others, you're creating a ripple effect that reflects back to you, nourishing your own heart and mind.

Sending love and peace is a deeply transformative practice for **your own emotional well-being**. It's about intentionally radiating these calming energies to create a harmonious space for yourself, no matter where you are.

How Love and Peace Influence Your Life

- **Deepening Your Connections**
  When you consciously send love and peace to others, you deepen your emotional connections. These feelings help you bond on a deeper level—not just through words or actions, but through a shared emotional experience. Over time, this practice fosters mutual understanding, care, and a sense of genuine connection. By sending love and peace, you're enhancing your own relationships, creating stronger, more meaningful ties with others.

- **Cultivating Harmony in Challenging Situations**
  Sending love and peace is incredibly powerful in difficult or tense moments. When you encounter conflict or stress, these emotions act as a grounding force for you. They help you stay calm, non-reactive, and centered. In doing so, you naturally influence those around you to remain more peaceful as well. This creates a safer emotional environment and allows conflicts to resolve more smoothly, helping you maintain control over your emotional state and encouraging harmony even in tough situations.

- **Building Emotional Resilience**
  By sending love and peace, you're strengthening your own emotional resilience. These feelings help you stay balanced and centered, regardless of what's happening around you. When you approach challenges with a peaceful mindset, you're more likely to stay calm under pressure, reducing the impact of stress. This allows you to respond with clarity and grace, rather than reacting impulsively. It's an empowering practice that builds your inner strength and emotional stability.

- **Enhancing Your Energy Field**
  As you continue to send out love and peace, these emotions naturally

raise your vibrational frequency. You may begin to notice that people are drawn to your positive, peaceful energy. Not only will you attract more harmonious situations, but you will also strengthen your personal power. You become less affected by external stresses and more in control of the energy you project. You're no longer just reacting to the world around you—you're creating a peaceful, loving energy that influences your surroundings.

The Ripple Effect of Love and Peace

Love and peace are high-frequency emotions that naturally dissolve tension and create an atmosphere of calm. They are some of the most powerful tools for building emotional connection because they transcend barriers—whether those are time, space, or the context of your interactions. By sending love and peace, you not only offer others a sense of care, but you also invite inner tranquility into your own life.

In addition, love and peace can have a broader impact on your environment. In spaces where you may not have direct influence, such as large groups or public areas, your energy can still shift the emotional tone of the room. As you practice these emotions consistently, they become ingrained in your interactions, making your connections with others feel more peaceful, loving, and fulfilling.

By embracing the practice of sending love and peace, you elevate not just your emotional state but the overall energy of your life, creating deeper connections, a stronger sense of resilience, and a more harmonious world around you.

Embracing Love and Peace in Action

Let's go over a few key points.

Are you listening?

Good.

Imagine you're at work, and you receive an email with challenging news—a stressful deadline or unexpected project. The immediate response might be frustration, stress, or worry, but instead of reacting with those emotions, you decide to pause. You take a deep breath and, as you read the email, silently offer love and peace to the situation. You acknowledge that this is a difficult moment, but you choose to face it with peace in your heart and love for the growth it could bring. You might even send thoughts of peace to the person who sent the email, understanding that they too are navigating their own challenges.

This energy of love and peace helps you stay grounded and focused amidst the stress. Rather than spiraling into anxiety, you transform the way you approach the challenge. You now feel a sense of calm, knowing that you have the ability to face this situation with clarity and grace. It's not about ignoring the stress, but about choosing to approach it from a place of inner peace.

Phase 4 is the natural extension of all the emotional practices you've built up to this point. Now that excitement, adventure, gratitude, and compassion are part of your emotional toolkit, it's time to take it a Phase further by introducing love and peace into your daily interactions. These two emotions are powerful forces that bring balance and unity to any situation.

By sending love and peace to those around you—whether directly or in your thoughts—you not only shift the energy of the moment, but you also contribute to a broader sense of harmony. It's not just about the person you're sending energy to; it's about what that energy does for you as well. Love and peace help you stay rooted in your highest emotional states, even when you encounter stress, conflict, or unexpected challenges.

Repeating Examples of Embracing Love and Peace

- **Walking Through a Busy Shopping Center**
  You're at a bustling shopping center, and people are rushing around, many of them looking stressed or impatient. Rather than absorbing the chaotic energy, you take a moment to pause. You silently send love and peace to everyone you encounter, wishing them a peaceful experience, whether they're in a hurry or simply browsing. You visualize the energy around you calming, everyone feeling more relaxed and present in their moment. This subtle shift in energy not only raises *your* energies, but helps create a more peaceful atmosphere for those around you as well.

- **In a Meeting at Work**
  During a meeting, tensions start to rise as differing opinions clash. Instead of getting pulled into the stress or frustration of the moment,

you silently center yourself and send love and peace to everyone in the room. You focus on creating a calm, harmonious atmosphere, wishing everyone clarity and understanding in their responses. *Your* energy shifts the dynamic, helping everyone to communicate more effectively and with a greater sense of mutual respect. As you remain centered, you help guide the conversation toward a more productive and peaceful resolution.

- **At a Party or Social Gathering**
  At a social event, you notice a conversation that's becoming a bit uncomfortable—perhaps there's tension or a disagreement brewing. Instead of getting caught up in the situation, you choose to send silent love and peace to everyone involved. You focus on the idea that everyone is just doing their best, and you silently offer thoughts of compassion and peace. This energy helps diffuse the situation, and even if it doesn't change everything right away, you've contributed to the overall atmosphere of calmness and understanding in the space.

- **At Home After a Stressful Day**
  You return home after a challenging day—perhaps feeling drained or frustrated. As you Phase through the door, you pause before entering your space. Instead of bringing the stress of the day with you, you take a deep breath and consciously send love and peace to your home. You visualize your space as a sanctuary, filled with calm and positive energy. This practice shifts *your* emotional state, and by the time you walk into the living room, you feel a greater sense of relaxation and presence. The energy you bring into the home influences the mood of those around you, creating a more peaceful environment for everyone.

Remember:

- **Don't Beat Yourself Up**
  Perfection is not the goal. You don't need to master the practice immediately. Sometimes you'll forget to pause and shift your emotional energy in the moment, and that's completely fine. What matters is that you're committed to practicing and growing. Each

attempt is a Phase forward, and each moment is a new opportunity to try again.

- **Patience is Key**
New practices take time to integrate, and sometimes it may feel awkward or forced. Trust that with patience, these emotions will naturally become a part of your daily life. Be consistent and gentle with yourself as you cultivate love, peace, excitement, and other positive emotions. Over time, you'll notice subtle but profound shifts in how you engage with the world.

- **Focus on the Process, Not the Outcome**
Rather than obsessing over immediate results, celebrate the small victories along the way. Notice moments when you successfully shift your emotional energy, even if it's just for a few seconds. Focus on the process of emotional engagement, and trust that the outcome will unfold over time. Each small shift in energy is a Phase toward greater emotional harmony.

- **Embrace Impermanence**
Emotions ebb and flow. Some moments will feel easier than others, and that's okay. When you experience negative emotions, acknowledge them without judgment and return to your practice. Recognizing that all emotions are temporary helps you approach each moment with greater self-compassion.

- **Trust the Long-Term Benefits**
The benefits of practicing the Front Door Activity will grow gradually. Emotional resilience, peace, and loving energy won't happen overnight, but with consistent practice, they'll become a lasting part of your life. Trust the process, knowing that the small shifts you make today will compound over time.

A Shift in *Your* Mindset

The most immediate change you'll experience is a **shift in perspective**. Rather than approaching your daily activities as mere tasks or routines, you'll start to see them as opportunities for connection, growth, and positive engagement.

- **Example**: Walking out the door in the morning no longer feels like a routine; it's an **opportunity** for something exciting to happen. Whether it's a meeting, a conversation, or a simple errand, you'll approach these moments with curiosity and openness.
- **How it feels**: You'll start noticing that your days feel more dynamic, and you'll become less focused on what's "wrong" or "negative" around you. Instead, you'll start to appreciate the **small joys**—whether it's the energy of a new experience or the satisfaction of a simple, peaceful moment.
- **Your life is now filled with gratitude, compassion, adventure and excitement**. Together these are... Love.

Embrace the Journey

The Front Door Activity is a practice of transformation, and it's not about perfect execution—it's about presence, consistency, and emotional growth. By incorporating love and peace into your daily interactions, you're cultivating a deeper connection to yourself and others. Every moment is an opportunity to engage in emotional transformation, making life feel more vibrant, connected, and full of potential.

Every door you walk through, every moment of emotional engagement, is an opportunity to practice love and peace. As you continue on this journey, you'll find that your emotional state becomes more balanced, resilient, and deeply rooted in positivity.

The Front Door Activity Does Not Make You 'Soft'... It Makes You Happier, More Efficient, Productive, and Results-Oriented

When people first encounter the **Front Door Activity**—a practice that emphasizes emotional mindfulness, the cultivation of positive energy, and intentional shifts in how you approach each moment—they might think it's about becoming "soft," passive, or overly focused on feelings at the expense of getting things done. However, this couldn't be further from the truth.

The reality is that **embracing love, peace, gratitude, and compassion** doesn't make you weaker; it actually strengthens your emotional resilience, mental clarity, and overall effectiveness. Far from being "soft," this practice makes you **more efficient, productive, and laser-focused on results**, all while maintaining a deep sense of emotional balance. Here's why:

Emotional Resilience Fuels Productivity

When you consciously engage with emotions like love and peace, you're building emotional **resilience**—your ability to stay centered, grounded, and focused in the face of challenges. In a world where stress, distractions, and setbacks are inevitable, emotional resilience is the cornerstone of productivity.

Why it works:

- When you're emotionally resilient, you're less likely to be derailed by external stressors or negative emotions.
- You can move through challenging moments without letting frustration or anxiety take up valuable mental energy.
- Your mental clarity improves because you're not caught in spirals of negativity or stress. Instead, you're able to focus on solutions and progress.

Example:

Imagine you're working on a tight deadline and a problem arises that seems like it could derail everything. If you're not emotionally resilient, you might panic, feel overwhelmed, and lose focus. However, if you've been practicing the **Front Door Activity**, you're better equipped to handle the stress. You pause, breathe deeply, and shift your emotional state to peace and calm. Instead of reacting in frustration, you think clearly and take immediate action to resolve the issue.

Positive Emotions Increase Efficiency

While it may seem counterintuitive, positive emotions—such as excitement, gratitude, compassion, and especially love—actually **boost**

efficiency. Positive emotional states **fuel motivation** and creativity, enabling you to approach tasks with energy, enthusiasm, and focus.

Why it works:

- **Positive energy** makes it easier to stay engaged and motivated, reducing procrastination.
- When you're feeling **grateful or excited**, you're more likely to approach challenges with a mindset of opportunity rather than a burden.
- **Love and compassion** foster collaboration and connection, which means you're more likely to work well with others and move projects forward efficiently.

Example:

You're working with a team on a project that requires creativity and collaboration. Instead of focusing on the stress of deadlines or the potential for conflict, you choose to send positive energy to the group—offering compassion, love, and peace. This shifts the dynamic in the room, making everyone feel more connected, valued, and motivated. The team works more harmoniously, brainstorming ideas with enthusiasm and solving problems faster, resulting in quicker and more efficient progress.

Reduced Emotional Reactivity Leads to Better Decision Making

One of the most significant benefits of sending love and peace to others and yourself is the reduction in **emotional reactivity**. When you become emotionally self-aware, you reduce the chances of making decisions based on knee-jerk reactions or impulsive emotions like frustration, anger, or fear. This means you're more likely to make decisions based on rational thinking and long-term goals.

Why it works:

- When you approach each situation with love and peace, you're able to remain **calm and clear-headed**, even when things get stressful.
- **Emotional awareness** gives you the ability to choose your responses

carefully, rather than letting external circumstances dictate your emotions.

- When you're not constantly reacting emotionally, you can think strategically, make better decisions, and stay focused on achieving your goals.

Example:

You're faced with a tough decision at work—a potential conflict with a colleague or a strategic challenge in a project. Instead of reacting impulsively out of frustration or fear, you take a moment to center yourself. By sending love and peace to the situation, you create a calm space to think critically about the best course of action. As a result, you make a more measured, well-thought-out decision that aligns with both your personal values and the overall goals of the team or company.

A Positive Mindset Helps You Maintain Momentum

One of the key factors in achieving **long-term success** is maintaining momentum—pushing forward even when faced with obstacles, setbacks, or exhaustion. A positive mindset, fostered by love and peace, is the fuel that keeps your momentum going.

Why it works:

- **Positive emotions** prevent burnout by keeping you energized and enthusiastic about your work.
- By focusing on excitement and the adventure of progress, you're better able to **persevere** in the face of challenges.
- A mindset of love and peace fosters **optimism**, which means you can see opportunities in challenges rather than focusing on the negatives.

Example:

You're in the middle of a long-term project that's starting to feel monotonous. Instead of getting bogged down by fatigue or frustration, you take a moment to shift your energy to excitement and peace. By reminding yourself of the larger purpose behind the work, you stay motivated and energized to finish the project strong. The energy you cultivate helps keep your momentum going, even when things get tough.

Fostering Better Relationships Enhances Collaboration and Results

The **Front Door Activity** focuses not only on your emotional state but also on how you interact with those around you. By sending gratitude, compassion, love, and peace to others, you cultivate stronger, more positive relationships, whether personal or professional. This ultimately enhances collaboration and creates an environment conducive to achieving results.

Why it works:

- **Fostering positive relationships** helps create a network of support, collaboration, and trust, which is essential for tackling ambitious projects.
- When people feel **seen**, **valued**, and **understood**, they are more likely to be cooperative, engaged, and willing to contribute toward a shared goal.
- As your relationships improve, you find that tasks and projects progress **more smoothly**, with fewer misunderstandings and more efficient teamwork.

Example:

You're working in a team that's faced with a high-pressure situation. Instead of focusing on individual tasks, you choose to send love and peace to the group, ensuring that everyone feels supported and encouraged. By fostering a spirit of collaboration, the team works together more effectively, with a shared sense of purpose and trust. The positive energy makes it easier to problem-solve, overcome challenges, and reach your objectives faster.

Emotional Mastery Leads to Higher Achievement

The **Front Door Activity** doesn't make you "soft." In fact, it does the opposite—it **empowers** you to become more effective, productive, and results-oriented. By cultivating love, peace, and emotional resilience, you give yourself the tools to face challenges with clarity, make better decisions, collaborate more effectively, and maintain momentum through even the toughest times. These emotional shifts not only make you a **more grounded, happier, and confident person** but also turn you into a **more efficient, focused, and results-driven individual**.

So, remember: when you **send love and peace** to the world around you, you're not just making the world a better place—you're also **creating a more focused, productive, and successful life** for yourself.

The Front Door Activity in Action
Remember: Small Acts, Big Changes

The beauty of the **Front Door Activity** is that it is a **simple** practice with **profound** impact. You don't have to make sweeping changes to your life in order to experience the benefits. By **shifting your emotional energy** in small, consistent ways throughout your day—starting with something as simple as walking through a door—you'll create lasting change in your emotional landscape, your relationships, and your overall sense of peace.

As you continue practicing the **Front Door Activity**, you'll begin to experience a life that feels more **balanced**, **mindful**, and **connected**. It's a practice that, while small in action, is **huge in impact**. Every step, every doorway, and every interaction becomes an opportunity to shift your mindset and embrace a more positive, compassionate, and open way of being.

Activity in Action 1

A Day in the Life of an Office Worker: The Front Door Activity in Action

Imagine stepping into your day not as just another routine of meetings, emails, and deadlines, but as a series of **opportunities to engage** with excitement, gratitude, and compassion. The **Front Door Activity** helps you transform each moment—whether you're heading out the door to begin your day or stepping back into your home after a long day—into an experience that is intentional, meaningful, and full of possibility. Let's walk through a day in the life of an office worker using this practice, and see how the energy of excitement and gratitude changes the way you engage with the world.

Morning: Leaving the House with Excitement and Adventure

It's 7:30 AM, and the world outside your door is full of new possibilities. You've spent the night resting, and now it's time to greet the day. Instead of simply trudging through your morning routine, you consciously decide to **infuse your departure with excitement and adventure.**

Start with Breath

The first thing you do upon waking is breathe deeply. You take a few moments to center yourself with a few conscious breaths. As you inhale, you breathe in the **energy** of a new day, and as you exhale, you release any lingering feelings of sleepiness or tension. This helps you prepare not just your body, but your mind for the day ahead.

Pause and Set Your Mindset

Before stepping outside the front door, you pause. You close your eyes for just a few seconds and bring up a sense of **excitement** and **adventure**. Think about a time in your life when you felt truly alive—perhaps during a trip, an unexpected adventure, or a moment when something exciting happened. Tap into the feeling of **anticipation** and **curiosity**. Even if it was a small moment, the key is to reconnect with that openness to the unknown.

Open the Door with Anticipation

When you finally open your front door, step out with a feeling of **expectation**. You're not just walking into the same old day. Instead, you approach the world outside with an open mind, filled with the possibility that something new and exciting will unfold—whether it's a pleasant surprise in a meeting, a new opportunity at work, or a fresh connection with a colleague. This is a **new beginning**, and you're excited to embrace it.

Activate Your Energy

As you step outside, you feel the energy of **adventure** flowing through you. Your steps are purposeful, yet open, ready for whatever comes your way. The world is no longer mundane. It's an exciting playground, full of opportunity, and you're prepared to engage fully with whatever unfolds. Whether you're heading to the office, the gym, or a coffee shop, you approach it with a mindset of **adventure**—ready to engage with whatever surprises the day might bring.

Example:

As you walk toward your car, you pass a neighbor whom you normally just wave at and keep walking. Today, however, you smile and feel that adventurous energy still buzzing within you. You decide to pause and say, "Good morning!" Instead of rushing off, you take a moment to chat, maybe about the weather or something new going on in the neighborhood. This simple interaction, which might otherwise have been overlooked, now feels like a meaningful connection. You embrace the opportunity, feeling that tiny moment could be enriching in its own right.

Why This Works:

By consciously shifting your emotional energy as you **leave the front door**, you've already set the tone for your entire day. **Excitement and adventure** are the foundation that helps you stay open to new possibilities. When you approach the world with this mindset, your day becomes more than just a series of tasks and obligations—it becomes an adventure filled with opportunities.

The more you practice this approach, the more you start to notice previously overlooked moments. What might have felt mundane before now becomes an opportunity for engagement, connection, and growth. **By starting your day with excitement, you activate an energy of openness** that will carry with you into every encounter, challenge, and opportunity.

Entering the Office: Gratitude and Compassion

You've made it to the office, and now it's time to shift your mindset once again. The transition from your home to your workplace can sometimes feel rushed or automatic—maybe you're thinking about emails, meetings, or tasks that await you. But today, you approach this moment with **intention**, choosing to bring **gratitude** and **compassion** into your experience. By practicing this mindful transition, you set a tone of warmth and understanding not only for yourself but also for those you encounter throughout the day.

Pause and Appreciate Your Surroundings

Before you step through the office door, take a brief pause. You might stop for just a few seconds on the sidewalk, by the entrance, or even as you walk through the parking lot. **Close your eyes** for a moment, breathe deeply, and bring awareness to your surroundings. **Appreciate the building**—the place that gives you the opportunity to work, collaborate, and make a living. Feel a sense of gratitude for this space that serves as your professional environment, even if it's not perfect.

It could be easy to focus on the noise, the busy schedule, or the discomforts of the workplace. But today, you consciously choose to **shift your focus** and appreciate the positives—the fact that you have a place to work, a community of colleagues, and the chance to contribute to something bigger than yourself.

Feel Gratitude for Your Job and Opportunities

Now, think about why you're grateful for your job. Whether it's the **income** it provides, the **sense of purpose** it offers, or the **personal growth** that happens along the way, take a moment to reflect. It could be the satisfaction of solving problems, the opportunity to learn new skills, or the chance to make a difference in your field.

Remember that **gratitude is an active choice**. Instead of focusing on frustrations, office politics, or challenging aspects of the job, you actively choose to appreciate the parts of your job that bring value to your life. Maybe it's the flexibility you enjoy, your supportive colleagues, or the stability the job offers. Holding this sense of **thankfulness** grounds you in the present moment and shifts your energy from lack to abundance.

Integrate Compassion into the Moment

As you approach the office door, you carry with you not only gratitude but also **compassion**—for yourself, for your colleagues, and for the many unseen people who make your workplace function smoothly.

- **Compassion for yourself**: Recognize the effort it takes to show up each day, to bring your best energy to work, even when you're tired, stressed, or dealing with personal challenges. Understand that you, too, are worthy of kindness and care.
- **Compassion for your colleagues**: Every person in your office is navigating their own journey. They may be facing challenges, even if they aren't immediately visible to you. Compassion helps you avoid jumping to conclusions or reacting to their energy. Instead, you see them as humans with their own struggles, and you approach them with understanding.
- **Compassion for the building staff**: The people who keep the office running—whether it's the cleaning crew, security personnel, or receptionists—often work in the background. But today, you acknowledge them too. They contribute to the smooth operation of your workplace, and showing them **gratitude and compassion** can make a huge difference.

Hold Gratitude and Compassion as You Enter

Now, as you step through the office door, you carry this energy of **gratitude** and **compassion** with you. As you walk through the entrance, you are not just entering a building—you are entering a space filled with human beings, all with their own stories, dreams, and struggles. You choose to remind yourself that everyone is navigating their own path, and by holding space for both your own and others' experiences, you contribute to a more harmonious and positive environment.

Example:

You walk into the office and notice a colleague rushing through the door, clearly stressed and overwhelmed. Normally, you might brush past them or even feel irritated by their energy. But today, you pause for a moment and **silently wish them well**. Instead of letting their tension affect you, you choose to **send them a thought of support**: *"I hope their day improves. I hope they find a sense of calm."* You might even send them a quick message through chat, something like: "Hey, how's everything going? Let me know if you need anything." Even if they don't respond immediately, the simple act of **offering support** can make a big difference—not just for them, but for your own sense of peace and connectedness.

Why This Works:

By consciously practicing **gratitude and compassion** as you arrive at the office, you create a positive and peaceful energy—not just for yourself, but also for those around you. These emotions are incredibly powerful because they ground you in appreciation for the present moment and for the people you work with.

- **Gratitude** helps you shift away from any feelings of lack or dissatisfaction. It allows you to see the abundance that already exists in your life and workplace. The simple act of **appreciating** what you have can change your perspective and boost your mood.
- **Compassion** fosters understanding and empathy. It allows you to connect with others on a deeper level, recognizing that each person has their own unique challenges. When you practice compassion, you're less likely to judge, react, or become frustrated by others' behaviors. Instead, you approach them with understanding, which can help reduce tension and create a more collaborative and harmonious environment.

By holding both **gratitude and compassion** as you enter the office, you create a peaceful atmosphere not just for yourself but for those around you. **You set the tone for the day**, creating a more positive, supportive, and connected workplace. Your interactions with colleagues may feel lighter, your presence more calming, and your connection with others more authentic.

Ripple Effect: Modeling Positivity

As you intentionally practice these emotions, you begin to **model them** for those around you. When your energy is one of gratitude and compassion, it has a **ripple effect** on the people you interact with. They may begin to respond in kind, making the entire work environment feel more supportive and positive. By shifting your energy, you contribute to a **more harmonious atmosphere**, where empathy and understanding become the norm, not the exception.

This practice also helps to **reduce stress and negativity** in the workplace. Instead of contributing to office politics or frustration, you become a force for **calm, kindness, and support**. This allows you to navigate challenges with greater ease and to handle workplace dynamics with grace.

The Power of Gratitude and Compassion

The simple yet profound practice of **gratitude** and **compassion** as you enter your office can have a powerful impact on your emotional state, your productivity, and your relationships with colleagues. It's not about ignoring the challenges or frustrations you might face; rather, it's about shifting your energy so that you approach each moment with a mindset that fosters positivity, understanding, and connection.

By making this transition from **excitement and adventure** when you leave home to **gratitude and compassion** when you enter the office, you are practicing emotional resilience. You are creating a work environment that reflects your inner peace, and you are contributing to the collective energy of your workplace. This is how small, intentional shifts in your energy can create a **larger impact**—one that not only enhances your own work experience but also influences the culture around you in meaningful ways.

During the Day: Sending Energy Out to Others

As you continue throughout your day, you actively practice **sending positive energy** to those around you. By intentionally carrying the emotions of **excitement, gratitude, compassion, and peace** into every interaction, you not only improve your own experience but also influence the atmosphere of the workplace. These small shifts can transform even the most ordinary interactions into opportunities for connection and positive energy.

Walking into a Meeting Room: Excitement and Adventure

Before entering any meeting, pause for a moment at the door. Take a deep breath and imagine that this meeting is an opportunity for **growth** and **collaboration**, regardless of how routine or potentially tense it might feel. Picture the team coming together with enthusiasm and creativity, open to new ideas and positive solutions.

Energy to Send: Feel the energy of **excitement** and **adventure** filling your mind. Visualize the meeting as a chance to engage with new perspectives, learn from others, and contribute positively.

Action: As you walk into the room, you bring this energy with you, allowing it to radiate from your presence. You may smile as you enter, letting that positive energy ripple outward. This will not only set the tone for the meeting but also subtly influence the mood of your colleagues, encouraging them to approach the conversation with openness.

Talking to a Colleague at the Coffee Machine: Gratitude and Compassion

As you chat with a colleague at the coffee machine or during a casual conversation, bring your **gratitude** and **compassion** into the moment. When they share details about their work or personal life, listen attentively, appreciating the opportunity to connect with them. Recognize that even in mundane office interactions, there is value in the exchange, and everyone has their own story and struggles.

Energy to Send: Be **grateful** for their insights and experiences. Offer **compassion** for their challenges, even if they're not explicitly shared. In your mind, wish them well in their endeavors, and acknowledge their personal journey.

Action: Instead of simply nodding along or offering a perfunctory response, allow your presence to show that you are truly engaged and caring. Acknowledge their emotions, empathize with their perspective, and offer support or encouragement where possible. You may even express a kind word like, "That sounds like an exciting project, I'm sure it's going to be great!" or "I can imagine how challenging that must be, hang in there."

Passing Someone in the Hallway: Gratitude and Compassion

As you pass a colleague, whether in the hallway, in the elevator, or in the shared office space, **send them silent gratitude and compassion.** You don't need to speak or do anything outwardly; it's more about the **intent** behind your actions. In that brief moment, recognize that they are human beings, with their own experiences, challenges, and joys.

Energy to Send: Gratitude for the simple fact that they are a part of your work life and **compassion** for whatever they may be experiencing at that moment. You can silently wish them **peace** or **ease** as they move through their day.

Action: Even though you may not have time for a lengthy conversation, your energy can still leave a positive mark. As you pass by, you may offer a friendly smile or a small gesture of acknowledgment. Your positive intentions will **subtly influence** the environment around you, making it more pleasant and supportive.

Why This Works:

By consistently sending out positive emotional energy to others in the workplace, you gradually transform your **internal environment** and the **external environment.** Here's how it works:

- **Magnetizing Positive Energy:** The more you consciously send **gratitude, compassion**, and **excitement** into the world, the more you attract these energies back to you. People tend to respond to kindness and positivity with warmth, and you will begin to notice that colleagues are more willing to collaborate, smile, or engage with you openly.

- **Building Stronger Connections:** When you show genuine compassion and interest in others' experiences, it deepens your connection with them. Even casual interactions become meaningful, and over time, this fosters a culture of empathy and mutual respect in the office.

- **Creating a Ripple Effect:** Your positive energy doesn't just stay with you; it influences the people around you. As you send out gratitude and compassion, others feel it, and they may begin to mirror these same emotions in their own interactions. This creates a **ripple effect** of positivity that can shift the overall atmosphere of your workplace for the better.

- **Embodying Presence:** By actively engaging with the people around you with intention, you become more present in your interactions. This creates a feeling of **connectedness** and **shared humanity**, which is essential for creating a healthy, supportive work environment.

Example in Action:

Let's say you're having a difficult morning, and you're feeling a little frazzled. When you enter the office and pass by a colleague in the hallway, instead of getting lost in your own stress, you pause for a moment and send them gratitude and compassion. You silently wish them peace and hope they are having a good day. You might even add a smile or a quick "Good morning!" as you pass them.

Later in the day, you attend a meeting where tensions are running a bit high. Before you walk into the meeting room, you take a deep breath and bring in that same excitement and adventure energy. As you sit down, you make a conscious effort to smile and approach the conversation with the belief that this is an opportunity to solve problems and collaborate creatively. By doing this, you subtly shift the energy in the room, and others may follow your lead, softening the tone of the discussion.

Throughout the day, by **intentionally sending energy out** to others in the form of **gratitude, compassion, excitement, love** and **peace**, you influence your environment and interactions in a positive way. These small acts can have a **profound impact** on the way you experience your day and the way others respond to you. It's a simple but powerful practice that fosters connection, kindness, and mutual understanding in every space you enter.

Lunch Break: A Moment to Recenter

Lunchtime offers a valuable opportunity to **pause** and recalibrate your emotional energy. It's easy to get caught up in the momentum of the morning and start feeling fatigued, stressed, or mentally scattered by midday. The **Front Door Activity** can serve as a way to reconnect with a sense of **purpose, peace,**

or compassion, helping you recharge and reset before diving back into the afternoon.

Stepping Outside: Releasing and Re-centering

Before you leave the office building or step outside for a walk, take a **moment** at the door to pause and check in with yourself. What emotion would be most helpful to carry with you for the rest of your day? If you've been feeling energized and positive, you might want to continue with **excitement** or **adventure**. If you're feeling a bit drained or overwhelmed, a shift to **peace** or **contentment** may be more fitting.

Energy to Send:

- **Excitement or Adventure:** If you're feeling good and looking forward to your break, embrace the energy of **exploration**. Acknowledge that even a short walk or time outside can be an opportunity for relaxation or new inspiration.
- **Peace or Contentment:** If you're feeling fatigued or need a reset, choose **calm** or **centeredness**. Feel the weight of the morning lift off your shoulders as you walk into the day with a sense of balance.

Action: As you step outside, consciously **carry** this emotion with you. Whether it's a short walk or just sitting in a nearby park or café, allow the shift to anchor your mindset. Your lunch break doesn't have to be just a physical break—it can also be a mental and emotional reset.

At the Café: Sending Compassion to Others

If you stop by a café, and the barista greets you with their usual smile, take this moment to reflect on the **shared humanity** between you. Instead of just completing the transaction, pause for a moment to **acknowledge** them as a person—not just as someone serving you.

Energy to Send: Compassion and **gratitude** for the person in front of you. Recognize that they have their own unique life and challenges, just as you do. They might be having a great day, or they may be going through something difficult. Sending compassion helps you see the connection between you and everyone you encounter, even in these seemingly small moments.

Action: Smile and look them in the eye. Rather than just ordering your usual, make it a point to say, "Thank you for the great service today," or, "I really appreciate you." These small gestures can **lighten** their day and add a layer of human connection that might not otherwise exist in the rush of a typical workday.

Bringing Compassion into Conversations

As you sit at the café or during your lunch break, you may have brief conversations with others. Whether it's a colleague joining you or a stranger sitting next to you, take a moment to acknowledge them as human beings with stories, experiences, and challenges of their own.

Energy to Send: Empathy and kindness. This doesn't mean offering solutions, but simply **being present** and showing an open heart. Even in a casual lunch conversation, you can create a moment of connection by listening with genuine interest.

Action: If someone shares something personal, whether it's about their weekend plans or a struggle they're facing, try to engage with empathy. A simple, "That sounds tough, I'm sorry you're dealing with that," or "That sounds like so much fun, I hope you enjoy it," can go a long way in making them feel seen and heard.

Example in Action:

Imagine you've stepped out of the office building to grab a coffee at a nearby café during your lunch break. As you walk to the counter, you notice the usual barista behind the counter—let's call him Alex. Instead of simply ordering your coffee as usual, you pause for a moment.

You silently think about how **grateful** you are for this small moment of peace, and how much you appreciate being able to step outside, enjoy some fresh air, and reconnect. You bring a sense of **compassion** for Alex, recognizing that their day might be filled with its own ups and downs, even if you don't know the specifics.

As you order, you look Alex in the eye, smile warmly, and say, "Thank you for making my coffee today. I appreciate your hard work." You see a slight shift in their expression—maybe a smile, maybe a bit of surprise at the genuine acknowledgment. In that moment, you've not only impacted your own mood but potentially made their day a little better, too.

Why This Works:

- **Resetting Your Energy:** Taking a moment to consciously center yourself during the lunch break helps to **recharge** your emotional batteries. Instead of rushing from task to task, you're actively choosing to bring fresh energy into your afternoon.
- **Cultivating Kindness:** Your small, mindful interactions at the café or with your colleagues help create a **positive ripple effect**. Compassion and gratitude don't have to be grand gestures—they're in the small, meaningful connections.
- **Strengthening Emotional Resilience:** By regularly practicing these emotional shifts, you begin to build emotional resilience. You're no longer at the mercy of external circumstances; instead, you're **training your mind** to shift and adapt, making you feel more balanced, grounded, and present no matter what happens during your day.

Lunch breaks are a perfect time to **recenter** and consciously decide what emotional energy you want to carry forward into the afternoon. By practicing gratitude, compassion, and the occasional shift to peace, you can **recharge emotionally** and influence those around you in a positive way. Whether you're walking through the door to grab coffee or simply taking a moment for yourself, using these practices can help you bring more **mindfulness** and **connection** into even the smallest interactions of the day.

End of the Workday: Gratitude for the Experience

The end of the workday can often feel like a rush to leave, as the mind starts to think of personal tasks, relaxation, or evening activities. However, the **Front Door Activity** offers a way to **close the day** with intention, reflection, and a sense of **gratitude**. This practice transforms the simple act of leaving the office into a moment of appreciation for everything you've experienced during the workday. It also sets you up for the evening ahead, bringing a fresh perspective into your personal time.

Pausing at the Office Door: Gratitude for the Day

Before you step out of the office, take a few seconds to pause. This is the moment to **reflect** on your day, recognizing both the good and the challenges you encountered.

Energy to Send: Gratitude. You can feel grateful for many things:

- **Your ability to contribute**: You made progress today, whether it was finishing a task, having a meaningful conversation, or learning something new.
- **The relationships you've nurtured**: Whether through collaboration, communication, or simply being a supportive presence, you've connected with others.
- **The growth you've experienced**: Every challenge—big or small—offered a lesson. Whether you overcame a difficult task or found a new way to handle stress, there's always something to appreciate.
- **The experience itself**: Work is often more than just a job; it's a place to stretch your skills, learn, and interact with people who shape your daily life.

Action: Close your eyes for a few seconds and reflect on these aspects of your day. You might even take a deep breath, inhaling the appreciation and exhaling any lingering stress or frustration. When you're ready, step outside, carrying this **gratitude** with you.

Walking Out: Excitement and Adventure for What's Next

As you leave the office and step out into the world, shift your emotional energy to one of **excitement** and **adventure**. The workday may be over, but the evening is full of opportunities and new experiences. This mindset invites a sense of **anticipation** for whatever the next few hours will bring, whether it's relaxing at home, socializing with friends, pursuing a hobby, or simply unwinding.

Energy to Send: Excitement and Adventure. Embrace the fact that your evening is a continuation of your day, and it holds the potential for something positive and fulfilling. The evening may not be filled with grand events, but it's still an opportunity to enjoy life in a new way.

Action: As you step away from the office, remind yourself that your journey isn't limited to your job. You're entering a new chapter of your day, and the possibilities are endless. Walk with your head held high, feeling ready for whatever comes next—whether it's relaxing or engaging in a creative project. The key is to approach it with the same energy of **adventure** and **openness** you had at the start of the day.

Example in Action:

Imagine you've just finished a busy workday. Your mind may be thinking about the tasks you completed, the meetings you had, or the issues that still need attention tomorrow. Instead of rushing out the door, you take a **moment** to pause.

You think about the things that went well today:

- You might have successfully completed a challenging task.
- Perhaps you had a meaningful conversation with a colleague that improved your working relationship.
- Maybe you faced a challenging project, but the process helped you grow and learn something valuable.

With each thought, you allow yourself to feel a wave of **gratitude** for the chance to engage in your work, for the experiences you had, and for the opportunities to learn.

As you step through the office door and into the world outside, you shift your focus to the evening ahead. Maybe you're looking forward to dinner with a loved one, a quiet evening with a book, or a fun event with friends. Whatever awaits you, you approach it with a sense of **excitement** and **adventure**, knowing that each part of your day offers something new.

Why This Works:

- **Closing the Day with Gratitude:** Pausing to reflect and appreciate your day helps to **center** your mind and heart. It can reduce feelings of stress or frustration from the workday, allowing you to leave the office on a **positive note**.
- **Shifting to Excitement for the Evening:** The energy of excitement and adventure keeps you **engaged with life**. It reminds you that no matter how routine the evening may seem, there is always something valuable waiting for you.

- **Creating a Balanced Mindset:** By practicing gratitude at the end of the workday, you're training your brain to notice the positive aspects of your experiences, leading to greater satisfaction and **emotional well-being**.

As the workday ends, use the **Front Door Activity** to **close your day** with a sense of gratitude and openness. Take a moment to reflect on your contributions, relationships, and growth before stepping out the door. Then, as you walk into the evening, bring with you the energy of **excitement and adventure**, knowing that the possibilities for relaxation, fun, or new opportunities are just beginning. By practicing this, you can transition from work mode into personal time with intention, carrying a positive mindset into whatever comes next.

The Evening: Returning Home with Gratitude and Compassion

After a long day, returning home can feel like a relief—especially when we've consciously shifted our emotional state during the day. The **Front Door Activity** offers a beautiful way to re-enter your personal space with intention, ensuring that the home you return to is filled with **gratitude, warmth, and emotional presence**. This step helps you ground yourself in the moment and reconnect with those around you, whether they are family, roommates, or even your own self.

Pausing at the Front Door: Gratitude for Home

When you arrive at the front door of your home, **pause for a moment** before stepping inside. As you stand at the threshold, take a deep breath and mentally recognize the blessings of your home.

Energy to Send: Gratitude. Reflect on the things that make your home a special place:

- **The warmth**: The feeling of being protected, whether from the cold or simply from the demands of the outside world.
- **The comfort**: The little things that make home feel safe and nurturing—your favorite chair, the soft bed, or even the kitchen where you prepare meals.

- **The people**: Whether you live alone or with others, home represents a place where you can be yourself, and that's worth appreciating.
- **The security**: Home offers stability, and it's a place of rest and restoration.

Action: Close your eyes for a moment and let that gratitude fill your heart. Appreciate the space and the comfort it provides. By stopping at the door, you're allowing yourself to **shift from the hustle and bustle of the outside world** to the peaceful sanctuary your home represents.

Entering with Compassion for Others

As you step inside, you bring with you a deep sense of **compassion** for the people who share this space with you. Whether it's your partner, children, family members, or roommates, each person you live with is on their own journey, facing their own struggles and triumphs.

Energy to Send: Compassion. Recognize that your loved ones are living through their own challenges, even if they're not immediately apparent. Their emotional state, experiences, and needs are just as important as yours, and by holding this awareness, you create an environment of **understanding** and **empathy**.

- **For family members**: You may have just come from a long day of work, but they've been navigating their own routines, perhaps with their own set of pressures.
- **For a partner or roommate**: They may have experienced highs or lows, and bringing compassion into your interactions allows you to approach them with a sense of kindness and emotional presence.

Action: As you greet them, take a moment to truly see them—not just as people you live with, but as individuals with unique needs, desires, and struggles. You might offer a soft "How was your day?" or simply smile, knowing that your emotional openness sets the tone for a compassionate exchange.

Example in Action:

You arrive home after a busy day at work. You pause at the door, and instead of rushing in, you take a moment to think about what your home represents to you. **Gratitude** fills your heart as you consider how fortunate you are to have a safe and comforting space to return to. You appreciate the little things—whether it's the familiar scent of your living room or the warmth of your home.

As you enter, your partner is sitting on the couch, looking tired from their own day. You feel **compassion** for them, knowing they've had their own set of challenges. You smile warmly and ask how their day was, knowing that their emotional well-being is just as important as yours. Your presence and kindness help to create a sense of connection and emotional safety in your shared space.

Why This Works:

- **Gratitude** shifts your focus from external demands and stressors to the abundance in your life. By practicing gratitude at the threshold of your home, you mentally reset, moving from the fast pace of the outside world to the calm and peace that home represents.
- **Compassion** opens your heart to the people around you. It allows you to interact with them in a way that acknowledges their humanity and their struggles, fostering a deeper connection. Compassionate energy also nurtures a harmonious environment where everyone feels understood and valued.
- **Emotional Presence**: By pausing and taking a moment to check in with yourself and those around you, you avoid rushing through your day. Instead, you allow yourself to be fully present with your surroundings and the people in your life. This presence cultivates **meaningful interactions** and strengthens your relationships.

As you return home at the end of the day, use the **Front Door Activity** to bring **gratitude** for the space you've created and **compassion** for the people you live with. By pausing for just a few moments before entering, you are setting the stage for a peaceful, grounded, and emotionally present evening. This small act of emotional intention transforms the way you interact with your home and loved ones, fostering connection, understanding, and a sense of belonging.

The **Front Door Activity** taps into the power of emotional intention, using the simple act of walking through doors as a way to transform your daily routine, your mindset, and your relationships. By consciously choosing to send positive energy—such as excitement, compassion, gratitude, or adventure—into the spaces you enter, you cultivate a mindset of **openness, positivity, and connection.**

Here's why this approach is so effective:

Shifting from Routine to Purpose:

We often rush through our daily routines without thinking much about our emotional state or the energy we're bringing into spaces. The Front Door Activity encourages you to pause before entering or leaving any space and consciously set an emotional tone for that moment. Instead of mindlessly going through the motions, you **reframe each experience** as an opportunity for positive emotional engagement. Whether it's at home, work, or even in public spaces, you begin to **see each door as a gateway to a fresh emotional opportunity.**

Fostering Connection with Others:

By consciously sending positive emotions to others, you enhance the quality of your interactions. Whether you're sending **gratitude** to a colleague or **compassion** to a family member, you're actively participating in creating a culture of kindness and understanding. **People are naturally drawn to positive energy** and are more likely to respond with warmth and openness. Even if you don't explicitly communicate these feelings, your energy and presence have a subtle yet powerful impact on the people around you.

Cultivating Emotional Awareness and Control:

The more you practice the Front Door Activity, the more you become attuned to your emotional landscape. You'll notice patterns in your emotional responses and begin to identify situations where you can intentionally shift your energy. For example, you might realize that you're feeling stressed before entering a meeting room, and you can choose to shift into a mindset of **excitement and adventure** instead of tension. This practice helps you gain greater **emotional awareness and mastery,** allowing you to **respond to situations rather than react impulsively.**

Creating a Ripple Effect of Positivity:

Positive energy is contagious. As you move through your day with intention and kindness, you create a ripple effect that impacts not just your own mood, but the mood of those around you. For example:

- You greet a colleague with **compassion**, which encourages them to open up.
- You approach your tasks with **excitement**, making even mundane activities feel fresh and fulfilling.
- You send **gratitude** to a stranger, helping to foster a positive interaction, even if it's just for a moment.

These small, intentional emotional shifts accumulate throughout the day, enhancing your relationships and creating a **more harmonious environment** wherever you go.

Uplifting Your Mood and Building Positive Momentum:

By focusing on emotions like **gratitude, excitement, and compassion**, you actively choose to **uplift your mood** and reframe challenging moments. If you're having a tough day or facing difficulties, the Front Door Activity provides a tool to **recenter** yourself. Instead of being weighed down by stress or frustration, you can choose to engage with the world from a place of **openness and positivity**. As you practice this, you'll begin to notice that your **mood** improves throughout the day, and you experience **more fulfilling interactions**.

Making Each Day Better:

The simple act of pausing at each door and setting an emotional intention transforms the way you experience your day. **Each moment becomes a potential opportunity** for growth, connection, and emotional transformation. Over time, you'll find that your routine becomes less of a grind and more of a **flowing experience of curiosity and mindfulness**. The impact of this small practice builds upon itself, creating a ripple effect that improves not only your emotional well-being but also the quality of your relationships and the way you engage with the world.

The Front Door Activity works because it **activates your emotional agency**, allowing you to consciously choose the energy you bring to each door, space, and interaction. By engaging with life through excitement, gratitude, adventure, or compassion, you reframe routine moments into meaningful opportunities for growth and connection. As a result, your mood improves, your interactions become more enriching, and the positive energy you cultivate extends to everyone around you, creating a ripple effect of kindness, positivity, and emotional presence.

Every door you walk through becomes an invitation to make your day better—not just for yourself, but for the world around you.

Bed Time:

Before heading to bed, you stand for a moment in your home—a space that represents your work, care, and love for your family. As you look around, you feel a deep sense of **gratitude** for the home you've created. You may think to yourself, *"I'm grateful for this safe space where my family can rest and feel loved."* You also acknowledge the work you put in today, both for yourself and your loved ones.

Perhaps you think, *"I'm thankful for the moments of connection I had with my children and partner, for the small victories in running the household, and for the opportunity to be present."* You pause to recognize that even the tougher moments—whether it was dealing with stress, managing a disagreement, or handling overwhelming tasks—are all part of your growth. In these moments, you send yourself **compassion**: *"It's okay that some things didn't go as planned. I did my best, and tomorrow is a new day."*

This reflection helps you release any tension from the day, bringing you into a state of emotional peace. As you walk away from the front door, you carry with you a sense of **gratitude and closure** for the day's experiences, knowing that every moment was part of the process of growth and connection. The challenges, the joys, and everything in between are all pieces of the beautiful mosaic of your life.

Closing the Day with Gratitude:

As you transition to the rest of your evening, you allow yourself to feel **grateful for yourself**—for the love, care, and attention you put into your home and family, and for how you've shown up in each moment. You may say a silent affirmation of appreciation, like: *"I'm grateful for today, for the love and work I put into my family, and for the opportunities I had to grow."*

By doing this, you end your day with a deep sense of **satisfaction, gratitude, and emotional peace**, knowing that no matter how the day unfolded, you've given your best. This practice of **reflection and gratitude** allows you to go to sleep with a heart full of appreciation for the day, preparing you to wake up ready to embrace tomorrow with a fresh perspective.

The Power of the Front Door Activity

By integrating the **Front Door Activity** into your daily routine, you're not just completing household chores or running errands—you are **transforming the mundane into something meaningful**. This simple practice invites you to engage with each moment intentionally, imbuing your daily tasks with energy, presence, and emotional connection. Whether you're folding laundry, cooking dinner, or just welcoming your family back home, each act becomes a powerful opportunity for growth, appreciation, and connection.

Instead of feeling like your day is a series of repetitive tasks or a never-ending cycle of responsibilities, you start to see every moment as a chance to **connect more deeply with yourself**, your loved ones, and the environment around you. The Front Door Activity encourages you to infuse your life with positive emotional energy—whether it's excitement, gratitude, compassion, or love—so that your home becomes a nurturing, energized space where every task holds purpose.

This shift in perspective means you're no longer just "doing"—you're **feeling**. By practicing intentional emotional engagement, your routine transforms from something to be endured into something you genuinely **cherish**. You begin to approach each day with a sense of **joy and gratitude**, even for the smallest things, and in doing so, your experience as a housewife becomes not only more mindful but also **empowering**.

Creating Sacred Moments

As you walk through the door of each room in your home, the act of crossing that threshold becomes a **sacred moment** of presence. Whether it's the front door to your home, the door to your children's rooms, or the kitchen door, each represents an opportunity to shift your emotional energy. You're not just entering a space—you're choosing to bring a specific emotion with you, enriching the environment around you.

For example:

- **Entering the kitchen**: Instead of thinking about the tasks ahead—dishes, cooking, cleaning—you can enter with gratitude.

Grateful for the food you're about to prepare, for the family that will eat it, and for the opportunity to nourish those you love.

- **Walking through the living room**: You might carry compassion, acknowledging that every family member has their own struggles, joys, and needs. This perspective shifts how you interact with them and how you care for the space itself.

Each moment, every door, is an invitation to live **more mindfully** and **emotionally engaged**, creating a positive and vibrant atmosphere in your home.

Building Connection with Yourself and Others

This practice also fosters **deeper connection**. By intentionally choosing emotions like gratitude, compassion, and excitement, you begin to enhance your relationship with yourself. You no longer feel overwhelmed by the demands of your day but rather see them as a part of a larger, more meaningful experience. You're actively **choosing how to engage emotionally** with your environment, which builds a sense of empowerment and control over your own life.

Moreover, your interactions with family members become more **attuned and heartfelt**. Whether it's greeting your partner with understanding or asking your child how their day went with genuine curiosity, you're showing up for them with emotional presence, which deepens your relationships.

A More Empowered Experience

At the end of the day, you'll notice the transformation that has occurred. The sense of **completion, connection, and fulfillment** will replace the feeling of "just getting through the day." You'll have created a day filled with energy, presence, and emotional engagement, fostering a sense of balance and harmony in your life. The Front Door Activity will have guided you through your routine with **purpose and meaning**, reminding you that every door you walk through is not just a physical passage, but an opportunity to engage with life in a more intentional way.

By embracing the power of the Front Door Activity, you become more **centered, grounded,** and connected to the beauty of the life you're creating—transforming not only your daily experiences but your entire mindset.

The **Front Door Activity** reminds you that you are the architect of your experiences. You can shape how you approach each day, and by choosing to bring positivity, **excitement, gratitude** and **compassion** into each doorway, you can make every moment count.

Now, your experience will not only be **mindful and present**, but **full of possibility**, adventure, and joy. Every door you walk through is a chance to experience life in its fullness.

Let's put it all together

A Full Day Using the Perfect Thought Activity, What Activity, Charisma Activity, and Front Door Activity

Let's walk through a typical day, integrating the **Perfect Thought Activity**, **What Activity**, **Charisma Activity**, and **Front Door Activity**. We'll see how a person can seamlessly apply each one of these activities throughout their day, from morning until night, incorporating work, social interactions, and daily tasks like shopping.

Morning: Starting the Day with Power and Purpose

Perfect Thought Activity (Morning Focus)

You wake up to the sound of your alarm. As you open your eyes, you notice a lingering thought: *"I'm too tired to get through today."* Instead of letting this negative thought take root, you apply the **Perfect Thought Activity**. You pause, take a deep breath, and repeat to yourself:

"This thought is perfect now."

You smile at the thought, acknowledging it without judgment, and then shift your energy. You replace it with a more empowering thought: *"I'm ready for today. I am fully capable of handling whatever comes my way."* This sets the tone for your morning.

Charisma Activity (Energy Activation)

Now, before you even get out of bed, you remember your **Charisma Activity**. You close your eyes, recall a moment when you felt truly **confident**—perhaps a time when you nailed a presentation or received a compliment. You draw that feeling of confidence into your heart, letting it expand.

Then, you imagine that confidence rising to your **third eye** and moving through your eyes like a beam of light. You send that confident energy out to your home, your family, and the day ahead. You mentally send out love

185

and strength to the people you'll encounter today, whether it's your coworkers, clients, or strangers on the street. By doing this, you are actively cultivating your charisma and radiating positive energy from the moment you wake up.

Front Door Activity (Excitement and Adventure)

As you step out the door to go to work, you take a moment to **apply the Front Door Activity**. Before you leave, you pause at the front door, take a deep breath, and mentally remind yourself:

"Today is full of excitement and adventure."

You frame your day as an opportunity to explore and engage with the world in a fresh and exciting way. You don't know exactly what will happen, but you're open to whatever new experiences come your way.

At Work: Handling Challenges and Interactions

What Activity (Dealing with a Challenge)

At work, you're hit with an unexpected problem. Your boss asks you to take on a challenging project you weren't prepared for. You feel a wave of anxiety and doubt: *"I'm not sure if I can handle this. What if I mess it up?"*

Instead of spiraling into anxiety, you immediately use the **What Activity**. You ask yourself a clear, solution-oriented question:

"What do I need to do to tackle this project successfully?"

Your brain starts processing. The response is clear:

- Research the project details.
- Break it down into manageable tasks.
- Ask for advice from a more experienced colleague if needed.

Instead of focusing on the uncertainty, you now have a roadmap. You act on the first step—researching the project—and feel more grounded and confident.

Charisma Activity (Confidence and Leadership)

Later in the day, you're leading a meeting. You want to be **charismatic**—to radiate confidence, authority, and leadership. You take a moment before the meeting starts, close your eyes, and invoke your **confidence energy**. You feel that surge of leadership rising from your core, and you mentally send out this energy to your colleagues.

As you speak, you feel your words landing with authority. You know what you're talking about, and your confidence is contagious. You visualize a light beam extending from your eyes, subtly influencing the room and engaging your coworkers. People respond positively to your presence and leadership.

Afternoon: Navigating Interactions and Personal Tasks

Front Door Activity (Gratitude and Compassion)

After a busy afternoon, you return home from work. As you open the door to your house, you pause and engage in the **Front Door Activity**. Before stepping inside, you take a moment to look around and bring a feeling of **gratitude** into your mind:

"I'm grateful for this place I call home. I have a roof over my head, food to eat, and a space to relax."

Then, you shift into **compassion** for those you live with—family members, roommates, or even pets. You recognize that everyone has their own struggles and experiences, and you mentally offer compassion to them.

What Activity (Self-Care and Reflection)

As you go about your evening routine, you feel a sense of overwhelm creeping in. You've had a long day, and you haven't had a chance to unwind yet. You use the **What Activity** to help you navigate this feeling:

"What do I need to do right now to take care of myself?"

Your mind offers a few clear responses:

- Take a 15-minute break to rest.
- Drink some water and relax with a cup of tea.
- Engage in a short, calming meditation.

You immediately act on the first step, giving yourself permission to rest for a bit.

Evening: Wrapping Up the Day with Gratitude and Personal Energy

Perfect Thought Activity (Nighttime Reflection)

Before you go to sleep, you reflect on the day. You notice that some negative thoughts from earlier in the day have crept back: *"I didn't handle everything perfectly. I could've done better."*

You apply the **Perfect Thought Activity**: You acknowledge these thoughts without judgment, smile at them, and say:

"That thought is perfect now."

You then replace it with a positive affirmation: *"I did my best today, and that's enough. I learned and grew, and I'm grateful for that."*

This helps you end your day on a peaceful note, free from self-criticism or regret.

Charisma Activity (Sending Love Before Bed)

Before you sleep, you do one last round of the **Charisma Activity**. You close your eyes, and this time, you bring a feeling of **love** into your heart. You send this energy to your loved ones, to yourself, and to anyone you interacted with during the day. You mentally send love to your coworkers, your family, and even to strangers you encountered.

As you drift off to sleep, you feel a sense of warmth and connection to everyone and everything, knowing that you've contributed positively to your own energy and to those around you.

Summary of How Each Activity Was Used Throughout the Day:

- **Perfect Thought Activity:** Used to shift negative self-talk into empowering thoughts, both in the morning and in the evening.
- **What Activity:** Used to focus on solutions and next steps when faced with challenges at work and in personal life, eliminating ambiguity and increasing clarity.
- **Charisma Activity:** Applied to cultivate personal energy (confidence, leadership, and love) before important interactions and throughout the day to influence those around you.
- **Front Door Activity:** Used to shift emotional energy when entering or leaving spaces, enhancing the experience of excitement, gratitude, and compassion as you interact with the world.

By incorporating these activities throughout the day, you align your emotional state, energy, and actions with the mindset of a modern guru. You become a more present, confident, and compassionate individual, capable of navigating the ups and downs of daily life with ease, purpose, and authenticity.

At the Gym or During Exercise

Perfect Thought Activity

You're struggling through a challenging workout, and your mind starts sending you messages like: *"I'm too weak for this. I can't finish."* Instead of succumbing to the negative thoughts, you apply the **Perfect Thought Activity**:

"This thought is perfect now."

You smile at the thought, accepting it as part of your experience, and then replace it with: *"I'm strong and capable. I can push through this."*

What Activity

As you push yourself further, a thought arises: *"Why am I so out of shape?"* Instead of dwelling on the "why," you ask:

"What can I do to improve my fitness?"

The answer is simple:

- Set a specific fitness goal (e.g., run a 5K in 3 months).
- Create a workout schedule.
- Monitor progress each week.

You begin by taking one small step toward action, such as signing up for a race or mapping out a workout plan.

Charisma Activity

While exercising in a public space (like a gym), you might feel self-conscious or unsure of yourself. Instead of focusing on your insecurities, you use the **Charisma Activity**. You think of **confidence** and imagine that energy emanating from your body. You mentally project that confident, strong energy to those around you—whether it's sending your energy to a fellow gym-goer or even the gym itself.

Front Door Activity

Before walking out the door to the gym, you remind yourself:

"This is an exciting adventure to grow stronger and healthier."

Upon returning home, you pause at the front door and bring up a sense of gratitude for your body's strength, even if it's a work in progress. You send compassion to yourself for the effort you've put in.

At a Family Dinner

Perfect Thought Activity

During a family dinner, you notice an old thought creeping in: *"I don't belong here. I'm different from everyone else."* You immediately use the **Perfect Thought Activity** to acknowledge it:

"This thought is perfect now."

You then replace it with: *"I am connected to my family, and we all have our own unique contributions."* This shifts your perception of the situation.

What Activity

You realize you're feeling disconnected and a little left out of the conversation. Instead of asking, *"Why does this always happen?"* you ask:

"What can I do to feel more engaged in the conversation?"

The answers are:

- Ask questions about what others are talking about.
- Share a story or experience you feel comfortable with.
- Simply listen attentively and offer a smile.

Charisma Activity

As the conversation continues, you decide to send out an energy of **love and compassion** to everyone at the table. You imagine that energy flowing from your eyes, wrapping around each family member, creating a space of warmth and connection.

Front Door Activity

Before leaving the dinner, you pause at the door and bring a feeling of **gratitude** for the food, the company, and the opportunity to spend time together. You also feel **compassion** for the experiences and struggles that each family member may be going through.

At Work (Handling Conflict)

Perfect Thought Activity

You get into a heated discussion with a colleague. A thought arises: *"I'll never get through to them. They don't understand me."* You immediately apply the **Perfect Thought Activity**:

"This thought is perfect now."

You then shift it to: *"I can communicate effectively. I can find common ground."*

What Activity

You're unsure how to approach the conversation and get your point across without escalating the conflict. Instead of asking *"Why don't they listen?"*, you ask:

"What can I do to communicate more effectively with them?"
The answers:

- Listen to their perspective first.
- Find a way to express your thoughts clearly and calmly.
- Focus on solutions, not blame.

You decide the next step is to take a deep breath and listen without interrupting.

Charisma Activity

As the conversation goes on, you notice tension in the room. You decide to send out **compassionate energy** through your eyes, offering empathy for the colleague's perspective. You imagine your energy connecting to them, softening the conversation.

Front Door Activity

When you leave the meeting, you pause outside the office and feel a sense of **gratitude** for having made it through the discussion. You also send **compassion** to your colleague, acknowledging that they, too, are doing their best.

During a Stressful Situation (Running Late or Overwhelmed)

Perfect Thought Activity

You're running late, feeling stressed out, and a negative thought pops up: *"I'll never get everything done. This day is ruined."* You pause and apply the **Perfect Thought Activity**:

"This thought is perfect now."
You then replace it with: *"I can handle this. I will do the best I can with the time I have."*

What Activity

You start to feel overwhelmed by your to-do list and wonder: *"Why is everything piling up at once?"* Instead of dwelling on the "why," you ask:

"What do I need to focus on right now?"

The answers are clear:

- Prioritize the most urgent tasks.
- Delegate what you can.
- Let go of perfectionism and just do your best.

You immediately take the first step: prioritizing your most urgent tasks and tackling them one by one.

Charisma Activity

As you work through your to-do list, you consciously choose to project **confidence** and **calmness**. You visualize these energies emanating from your body, helping you move through your tasks efficiently. If you have to interact with others, you send out this energy to them, maintaining your calm presence.

Front Door Activity

At the end of the day, you pause at your front door and feel **gratitude** for having made it through a challenging day. You reflect on the effort you put in and send **compassion** to yourself for all that you accomplished. You embrace the imperfections of the day and give yourself credit for pushing through.

Shopping or Running Errands

Perfect Thought Activity

You find yourself getting frustrated in a long line at the store. You think: *"This is wasting my time. I'm always stuck waiting."* You use the **Perfect Thought Activity** to release the frustration:

"This thought is perfect now."

You replace it with: *"I'm exactly where I need to be, and this moment is just fine."*

What Activity

While waiting in line, you feel impatience creeping in and ask yourself: *"What can I do to make the best of this situation?"*

The options:

- Use the time to relax and take a few deep breaths.
- Look for something new in your surroundings.
- Be present and enjoy the moment instead of rushing through it.

Charisma Activity

As you're checking out at the cashier, you decide to send out **love and kindness** to the person behind the counter. You smile and mentally send them positive energy, creating a positive interaction.

Front Door Activity

As you leave the store, you pause outside the door, taking a moment to feel **gratitude** for the items you purchased and the ability to meet your needs. You send **compassion** to the people in the store, acknowledging the challenges they may be facing in their lives.

Before Going to Bed

Perfect Thought Activity

As you lie in bed, you reflect on your day. You notice a lingering thought: *"I didn't get everything done. I didn't do enough."* You apply the **Perfect Thought Activity**:

"This thought is perfect now."

You then replace it with: *"I did the best I could today, and I am enough as I am."*

Charisma Activity

Before drifting off to sleep, you focus on **self-love**. You send a beam of loving energy to yourself, reminding yourself that you are worthy, capable, and deserving of peace.

Front Door Activity

You mentally imagine your front door as a symbolic threshold to the next day, where you can embrace gratitude and compassion for the opportunity to begin again. You mentally thank yourself for a day well-lived and look forward to the next.

BONUS ACTIVITY 1: The Power of the Breath

The Power of the Breath: A Comprehensive Guide to Conscious Breathing

Breathing is one of the most fundamental functions of the human body. It is the act that sustains life, and yet it often goes unnoticed. However, in times of stress, anxiety, or mental fog, the way we breathe can significantly affect how we feel. This is where **conscious breathing** comes in. Conscious breathing is a practice that encourages you to become aware of your breath and intentionally control it, helping you tap into the body's natural relaxation response. One such breathing technique is the **"3 In - 4 Out" method**, a simple yet powerful tool to help reduce stress, promote emotional well-being, and improve mental clarity. In this guide, we'll explore the benefits and steps involved in this conscious breathing activity, highlighting why it is so effective for everyday use.

Understanding the Breathing Cycle

Before delving into the specifics of this breathing activity, it's essential to understand what conscious breathing is and why it works.

Conscious breathing is the act of paying attention to your breath—how it enters and leaves your body. Breathing is something most of us do automatically, but by bringing our focus to the act of breathing, we can influence the autonomic nervous system, which governs bodily functions like heart rate, digestion, and stress response. The **parasympathetic nervous system**—also known as the "rest and digest" system—plays a crucial role in calming the body and mind. By intentionally slowing the breath and making it more rhythmic, we can activate this system, reduce stress, and promote relaxation.

The **"3 In - 4 Out" method** is a controlled breathing practice that focuses on a natural, relaxed inhalation and a slightly longer exhalation. This method emphasizes **normal breathing** (not deep or forced), making it accessible for people to practice anytime, anywhere.

Step-by-Step Guide to the "3 In - 4 Out" Breathing Activity

Step 1: Find a Comfortable Space

To begin, it's important to be in a place where you can focus without distractions. Find a comfortable chair or lie down on your back if you prefer. You don't need to sit cross-legged or assume any specific posture—just make sure your body feels at ease.

Step 2: Initial Relaxation Breaths

Start by taking a few **deep breaths** to settle into the moment. Inhale gently through your nose, hold for a second, and exhale slowly through your mouth. With each breath, allow your body to relax. Focus on releasing any tension you might be holding in your body, particularly in the shoulders, neck, and jaw. This phase is about gently calming your nervous system and preparing for the more structured breathing to follow.

Step 3: Begin the 3 In - 4 Out Breathing Cycle

Now, start the conscious breathing cycle. The idea here is to inhale through the **nose** for a count of **3**, then exhale through the **mouth** for a count of **4**. This means the exhalation is slightly longer than the inhalation, which is key to activating the parasympathetic nervous system.

- **Inhale through the nose for 3 counts.** As you breathe in, let your breath fill your lungs naturally, not deeply. Keep it relaxed.
- **Exhale through the mouth for 4 counts.** Let the exhalation be a little longer than the inhale, but again, do not force it. The exhale should feel relaxed and natural, just a bit extended.

Step 4: Repeat the Cycle

Begin by repeating this cycle **6 times**—that's 6 breaths in and 6 breaths out (3 counts in, 4 counts out). Focus on maintaining a smooth rhythm without rushing. As you breathe, feel the tension in your body release and your mind becoming quieter.

Step 5: Gradual Progression

As you continue the practice, try to extend the duration of the exercise. Start with 6 breaths, and over time, gradually work your way up to **5–6 minutes** of breathing. There's no need to rush; allow your body to adjust naturally to the rhythm. You might find that after a few days, you are able to increase the duration, while still maintaining comfort and relaxation.

Step 6: Practice Throughout the Day

While the initial recommendation is to practice this breathing exercise in the morning and evening (before sleep and after waking up), you can incorporate it at any time during the day. Whether you're feeling stressed at work, stuck in traffic, or simply need to regain focus, taking a few moments to breathe in this mindful way can help center you and reduce anxiety.

Why the "3 In - 4 Out" Method Is So Effective

The conscious breathing exercise described above is powerful for several reasons. It's a simple technique that anyone can use, but its impact on the body and mind is profound. Here are a few reasons why it's so effective:

Promotes Relaxation and Reduces Stress

The most significant benefit of this breathing technique is its ability to activate the **parasympathetic nervous system**, which is responsible for calming the body. By focusing on the exhalation being slightly longer than the inhalation, the body moves from a state of tension (associated with the **sympathetic nervous system**, or "fight or flight" response) into a more relaxed, calm state. This is particularly useful in times of stress or anxiety, as it encourages the body to slow down, which in turn helps to reduce feelings of being overwhelmed.

Improves Mental Clarity and Focus

The simple act of breathing with awareness also enhances **mental clarity**. When we are stressed, our minds tend to race, and it can become difficult to focus. However, as you focus on the rhythm of your breath—particularly on the slight elongation of the exhalation—the mind becomes quieter, and the body enters a state of **mindfulness**. This allows you to be more present and focused, whether you're working on a task or simply interacting with others.

Accessible and Easy to Practice

One of the key strengths of this method is that it involves **normal, relaxed breathing**, not deep or forced breaths. This makes it far easier to maintain throughout the day. People often feel that they can't practice breathing exercises because deep breathing can feel tiring or too intense. The "3 In - 4 Out" method, however, requires no special technique—just a gentle, natural rhythm. It is sustainable, meaning it can be practiced for long periods without discomfort.

Helps Regulate Emotions

By regulating the breath, you also regulate your emotional state. The practice of conscious breathing encourages **emotional regulation**, which is crucial for maintaining emotional balance. Whether you're experiencing anxiety, frustration, or even excitement, conscious breathing helps keep your emotions in check by fostering a state of calm and composure.

Can Be Done Anywhere

The beauty of this technique is its simplicity and versatility. Because the breathing is not deep or intense, it can be done in almost any setting—whether you're sitting at your desk, walking around, or lying in bed. It doesn't require a quiet space or specialized equipment, making it perfect for busy, on-the-go lives. Whenever you feel the need to reset or ground yourself, you can simply stop and take a few moments to breathe consciously.

Sustainable Practice for Daily Life

This breathing exercise can easily become a part of your daily routine. You don't have to carve out long periods of time for meditation or yoga (although those practices are beneficial too). Instead, you can practice conscious breathing throughout your day, whenever you need a break. Over time, it becomes second nature and an automatic response to stress.

The Power of the Breath

The "**3 In - 4 Out**" conscious breathing activity is a simple yet profound practice. By focusing on the natural rhythm of the breath and emphasizing a slightly longer exhalation, you activate your body's relaxation system, calm your mind, and regulate your emotions. The technique is not only powerful but also highly accessible, as it doesn't require deep breathing or special skills. Whether you use it at the beginning and end of your day or whenever stress arises, conscious breathing is a practical and sustainable tool for creating balance in your life.

This activity allows you to connect with your body and mind in a way that is both grounding and calming. By practicing mindful breathing, you open yourself up to greater mental clarity, emotional regulation, and a deeper sense of well-being. So, next time you feel stressed, take a deep breath (in the most natural way possible), and remember: the power of your breath is always available to help you reset and regain focus.

Final Breathing Advice

1. **If you find it difficult to sleep**, do your 3-4 breathing in bed at night. Start by practicing it for 1 minute, then gradually over a number of days build up to 5–6 minutes. This simple practice will help calm your mind and body, allowing you to sleep more soundly. With regular practice, it can become a natural way to ease into restful sleep.

2. **When you wake up in the morning**, keep your eyes closed and maintain that relaxed, sleepy state for two minutes. Practice your 3-4 breathing during this time. This will help you gently transition from sleep to wakefulness and provide a natural energy boost to start your day feeling refreshed and revitalized.

3. **When you feel stressed during the day**, slow down and take six 3-4 breaths. Your body will begin to relax, and your mind will sharpen, allowing you to regain focus and composure. Whether you're at work, in a meeting, or navigating a challenging situation, this simple practice can help you reset and approach the moment with greater clarity and calm.

BONUS ACTIVITY 2: Perfect for Procrastinators

K aizen: Perfect for procrastinators and when overwhelmed by big tasks

"The Kaizen Challenge"
Pick any one thing you've been avoiding and do it for 60 seconds.
Next day do it for 2 minutes.
Then for 3...
You get the drift

Procrastination is something that almost everyone has experienced at one point or another. Whether it's delaying an important project at work, putting off a workout, or postponing a tedious household chore, the tendency to avoid tasks that seem overwhelming or unpleasant can often feel like an insurmountable barrier. This is where **Kaizen**, a Japanese philosophy of gradual, continuous improvement, can become a game-changer for those who struggle with procrastination.

The Concept of Kaizen

The word *Kaizen* is derived from two Japanese words: *kai* (change) and *zen* (good or better). In its most straightforward translation, Kaizen means "change for the better," but it is often interpreted as "continual improvement." The philosophy of Kaizen encourages making small, incremental improvements over time, rather than aiming for a huge leap or drastic transformation all at once.

In business, particularly at Toyota, Kaizen has been a fundamental part of their approach to lean manufacturing, aiming to optimize efficiency by continuously refining processes through small but consistent improvements. However, the principles of Kaizen are just as applicable in personal development. Whether you're looking to improve your health, productivity, or any other aspect of your life, Kaizen can be a powerful tool in breaking down the barriers that often lead to procrastination.

The Procrastination Trap

Procrastination often stems from the fear or resistance to change. When a task feels large, overwhelming, or too difficult to begin, our minds tend to shut down or look for distractions. The brain is wired to avoid discomfort, so when we think about tackling something monumental, it can trigger feelings of anxiety, self-doubt, or a simple desire to avoid the stress altogether. This is why large, ambitious goals—like getting in shape, writing a book, or organizing a cluttered house—can often feel like insurmountable challenges.

One of the main reasons why New Year's resolutions, for example, often fail is because people set goals that are too big, too quickly. When they fall short or don't immediately see results, the motivation fades, and the procrastination cycle begins again. This is where Kaizen offers a more sustainable alternative.

Small Steps: The Kaizen Approach to Beating Procrastination

The central principle of Kaizen is to make change in small, manageable steps. Instead of trying to radically overhaul your entire life or take on massive tasks in one go, Kaizen advocates for breaking things down into tiny, incremental actions that seem so insignificant that your mind doesn't even have time to register the discomfort associated with change.

This method is especially effective for procrastinators, because small steps don't trigger the same fear response as larger, more daunting actions. Starting with something that seems almost too easy to matter allows you to bypass the mental resistance that typically leads to procrastination.

Kaizen in Action: One Minute a Day

One of the most effective ways to apply Kaizen to personal development is by setting a very small target: committing to just one minute a day of a desired activity. The goal is so tiny that it's nearly impossible to argue against it. The key is consistency—doing this small task every day, without fail.

Let's consider how this works with some common procrastination-prone activities:

Getting Fit

For many, starting a fitness regimen can feel like a monumental task. The thought of going to the gym for an hour or running five miles can seem overwhelming, and that's before you even get started. This is where the Kaizen approach comes into play. Instead of aiming for a 30-minute workout, you commit to something far more manageable: one minute of physical activity every day.

You could pace around your living room for one minute, walk to your mailbox, or take the stairs for one minute. It doesn't matter what the activity is—what matters is the consistency.

Once the one-minute routine becomes a part of your daily life, you may find that it's easier to extend the time. You might naturally start walking for two or three minutes, or even 20 minutes, without any additional effort. The important thing is that you are establishing the habit, and the small step prevents procrastination from taking over.

Cleaning and Household Chores

Many people find cleaning to be a daunting task, especially when the house is in disarray. It can feel like there's too much to do, so you put it off. But by applying the Kaizen principle, you can break the task down into much smaller steps.

For example, you could commit to vacuuming for just one minute each day. Instead of thinking about cleaning the entire house, which can be exhausting, you just focus on that one minute of vacuuming.

Similarly, if you need to clean out a cluttered garage or shed, the Kaizen approach suggests you start by putting away three items per day. That might take just a minute or two, but over time, these tiny efforts will add up. By the end of the month, you will have made significant progress with minimal stress.

Tackling Work or School Assignments

Procrastination is common when it comes to work or school projects, especially when the task feels overwhelming. Instead of staring at a large assignment and feeling paralyzed by it, you can start by working on it for just one minute each day.

One minute may not seem like much, but the key is to create momentum. Once you've spent a minute working on your task, you may find that it's easier to keep going. You may extend your time beyond that initial minute because you've already started. Over time, this will build into a habit of consistent work, and you'll likely finish the project without the stress and pressure that typically accompany procrastination.

Breaking Bad Habits

The Kaizen approach can also help break bad habits, such as smoking. If you want to quit smoking, for example, you could replace one cigarette per day with a healthier alternative, such as eating a piece of fruit or going for a brief walk outside. This small substitution may seem insignificant at first, but it begins to shift your behavior in a manageable way.

As time goes on, you can gradually replace more cigarettes with healthier alternatives. The small step-by-step process allows you to slowly reduce your dependence on the habit without feeling overwhelmed.

Learning Something New

If you want to learn a new skill or language, Kaizen can make this process much more approachable. Learning a new language, for example, can be intimidating, especially if you set a goal of becoming fluent in six months. Instead, try learning one new word or phrase each day. It takes only a minute, but over time, you'll accumulate hundreds of new words and phrases.

The same applies to any new skill. Whether it's playing an instrument, learning to cook, or developing a creative hobby, dedicating just one minute a day to the activity helps you slowly build competence and confidence without feeling like you're committing to a huge task.

The Power of Consistency

One of the most important aspects of Kaizen is the emphasis on consistency. It's not about making huge leaps or achieving instant results—it's about making small, steady progress. Over time, these little efforts compound into significant improvements.

This is especially beneficial for procrastinators, because the Kaizen method avoids the common pitfalls of perfectionism and overwhelm. You don't have to wait for the "perfect" time to begin, and you don't have to worry about getting everything right on the first try. Instead, you simply commit to showing up and taking small steps forward every day.

Small Steps, Big Results

Kaizen is a powerful tool for anyone struggling with procrastination. By focusing on small, manageable tasks, it allows you to avoid the mental barriers that often prevent you from getting started. The key is consistency—by taking just one minute a day, you'll gradually build positive habits and make lasting improvements in your life. Whether you're aiming to get fit, clean your house, or learn something new, Kaizen offers a simple, effective way to overcome procrastination and make meaningful progress without feeling overwhelmed.

In the end, the small steps add up, and what begins as one minute a day can eventually transform your life. So, next time you find yourself procrastinating, remember: just start with one minute. Your future self will thank you for it.

The Kaizen Challenge: Conquer Procrastination, One Small Step at a Time

We've all been there: staring at a task we know we need to do but finding every excuse to avoid it. Whether it's a work project, cleaning your house, exercising, or learning something new, procrastination can make even the simplest tasks feel overwhelming. But what if you could tackle any task, no matter how daunting, by taking it one tiny step at a time?

Welcome to **The Kaizen Challenge**—a simple, effective way to break through the barrier of procrastination and make progress, one small, consistent action at a time. The beauty of the Kaizen Challenge is that it taps into the power of tiny improvements and builds momentum, so you'll find yourself accomplishing more than you ever thought possible, with minimal stress and no overwhelm.

How The Kaizen Challenge Works

The Kaizen Challenge is based on the Japanese principle of Kaizen, which emphasizes making gradual, incremental improvements. The idea is to take one task you've been avoiding and break it down into small, manageable chunks—so small that it feels almost effortless.

The Challenge Process:

- **Pick One Task You've Been Avoiding:** Think about something that's been lingering on your to-do list, something that you've been putting off for days, weeks, or even months. It could be anything—something big like starting a fitness routine, tackling a work assignment, or cleaning out the garage, or something smaller, like making a phone call or sending an email.

The key is to choose something that feels significant to you but has been delayed due to procrastination or resistance.

- **Commit to 60 Seconds:** For the first day, commit to doing the task for **just 60 seconds**. The task should be small enough that you can easily fit it into a single minute. This first step is all about getting started—just taking action, no matter how small.

The brilliance of this first step is that **60 seconds** is so manageable, it feels almost silly to resist. Your mind can't come up with excuses, because the task is so short. For example:

- If you want to start exercising, walk around the room for one minute.
- If you need to work on a report, open your document and write one sentence or read one paragraph for 60 seconds.
- If your house needs cleaning, pick up three things and put them away for a minute.

The goal is to begin, no matter how small the action. **The key is consistency, not perfection.**

- **Increase by 1 Minute Each Day:** On the second day, commit to the task for **2 minutes**. On day three, you'll do it for **3 minutes**. The idea is to gradually increase the time you spend on the task by 1 minute each day.

The beauty of this method is that each incremental increase is so small it won't overwhelm you. As you build momentum, you'll start to feel less resistance and more motivation to keep going. You'll be surprised at how much progress you can make in a matter of days.

For example:

- On Day 1, you walked for 1 minute. On Day 2, you walk for 2 minutes.
- On Day 3, you may end up walking for 3 minutes and feel energized

enough to continue.

- On Day 4, you could be walking for 4 minutes, and before you know it, you're working up a full workout without the dread of committing to a long session from the start.

- **Keep Going:** As the days pass, you'll continue to add one minute each day. By doing this, you are building both the habit and your ability to tackle larger amounts of the task each day. What starts as a small, seemingly insignificant action grows into a sustainable and productive routine.

For example, if your original goal was to organize your garage:

- On Day 1, you might spend 1 minute putting things away.
- On Day 2, you spend 2 minutes.
- On Day 5, you're spending 5 minutes organizing and feeling a sense of accomplishment.
- By Day 10, you might be working for 10 minutes at a time, and soon enough, that overwhelming task becomes something you're actively engaging with every day.

Why This Works

- **Overcoming Mental Resistance:** Kaizen works by bypassing the resistance that typically comes with big changes. Our brains often resist major transformations, which is why big New Year's resolutions and drastic changes tend to fail. But when you focus on small actions, your mind doesn't have time to object. You're simply taking small steps, and each step leads to greater success.
- **Building Consistency:** One of the hardest parts of overcoming procrastination is simply getting started. The Kaizen Challenge eliminates the need to "gear up" or wait for the perfect time. With such a small commitment, you're bound to succeed, and that success breeds more success. Each day's small win encourages you to continue.

- **Creating Momentum:** Once you've committed to the task and taken the first step, it becomes easier to continue. Over time, the task will no longer feel as intimidating. As the time increases, you'll feel a natural flow and momentum that can carry you to even greater accomplishments.
- **Allowing Room for Imperfection:** Perfectionism often fuels procrastination. If we think a task has to be done perfectly, we might avoid it altogether. The Kaizen Challenge removes this barrier by allowing for small, manageable increments where perfection is irrelevant. You're simply showing up and making progress, no matter how small the step.

Kaizen Challenge Examples

Here are some examples of how you can apply the Kaizen Challenge to different areas of your life:

Fitness or Exercise:

- Day 1: Walk for 1 minute.
- Day 2: Walk for 2 minutes.
- Day 3: Jog for 3 minutes.
- Day 7: You could be jogging for 7 minutes or engaging in a full workout.

This gradual increase makes exercise less intimidating, and you'll feel proud of the consistency you've built.

Writing or Creativity:

- Day 1: Write for 1 minute.
- Day 2: Write for 2 minutes.
- Day 3: Write for 3 minutes.
- Day 5: You might find yourself writing for 10 minutes and generating a great idea.

Even if your goal is to write a novel or start a blog, the Kaizen Challenge helps you break through writer's block with just a few minutes each day.

Cleaning or Organizing:

- Day 1: Clean for 1 minute.
- Day 2: Clean for 2 minutes.
- Day 4: Tidy up for 5 minutes, focusing on one area.
- Day 10: You may find yourself cleaning and organizing for 15-20 minutes at a time, and your environment will feel vastly improved.

Learning a New Skill or Hobby:

- Day 1: Practice for 1 minute.
- Day 2: Practice for 2 minutes.
- Day 5: You could be practicing for 10 minutes, and after a week or two, you may have learned a new skill, whether it's playing an instrument, learning a language, or improving your cooking.

Breaking a Bad Habit (e.g., Smoking):

- Day 1: Replace 1 cigarette with a healthier alternative (like a piece of fruit or a walk).
- Day 2: Replace 2 cigarettes.
- Day 5: You may replace 5 cigarettes per day and feel less dependent on smoking.

Remember: Start Small, Achieve Big

The Kaizen Challenge is the perfect solution for anyone struggling with procrastination or feeling overwhelmed by big tasks. By starting with just 60 seconds, you can eliminate the fear and resistance that comes with starting something new. Gradually increasing the time each day builds both your habit and your confidence, making it easier to continue without burnout.

So, choose one task you've been avoiding, commit to just 1 minute today, and keep adding 1 minute each day. By the end of the challenge, you'll have made real, lasting progress—and, more importantly, you'll have broken the cycle of procrastination once and for all.

Are you ready to take The Kaizen Challenge? Start today, and see how much you can achieve with just one small step at a time.

CONGRATULATIONS! YOU'RE STILL A MESS

Epilogue

Well, here we are. You've made it through. You've stared your life in the face, examined your flaws, and accepted the responsibility to change. If you've done the work—if you've followed the rules and faced the fire—then you're not the same person you were when you started this book.

But don't get it twisted. This isn't the end. It's just the beginning. The game doesn't stop after you close this book. Life doesn't hand you an award just because you made it through a few chapters. The real work begins now. Every single day, you get to choose: do you keep playing the same old losing game, or do you step up and play it the right way?

I know it's tempting to slip back into your old ways. To ignore the work, to go back to the comfort of your old excuses. But that's the easy road. And easy doesn't get you what you want. Easy gets you more of the same—more of the noise, more of the distractions, more of the failure.

Here's the deal: you *will* fail. You'll slip up. You'll get angry. You'll question everything. But that's part of the game. You didn't think this was going to be a cakewalk, did you? There's no shortcut to success. There's no easy way out. But there is a way to keep moving forward, even when things get tough.

The truth is, life is never going to hand you a map. But now, you have a compass. Now, you know how to get where you want to go. Now, you know that the only thing standing in your way is your own mindset.

So here's the challenge: don't stop now. Don't let the work stop just because you finished reading these words. Every single day, you wake up with a choice: to keep playing the game by your own rules, or to let the world keep controlling the board. You've learned how to win—now it's time to show up and prove it.

This is your life. This is your game. And from this moment on, you are the one who decides how it's played. No more excuses. No more distractions. No more losing.

You've got this. But don't just take my word for it. Go out there and show the world.

Your move.

About Alex Telman

ALEX TELMAN IS A GLOBALLY recognized spiritual healer, author, and one of the country's most read poets. With over 45 years of experience, he has dedicated his life to helping individuals break free from negative energies, trauma, and spiritual blockages. His transformative work has empowered a diverse range of clients, including celebrities, business leaders, educators, and everyday individuals, guiding them toward emotional well-being, personal growth, and spiritual fulfillment.

From an early age, Alex demonstrated extraordinary abilities to perceive and remove harmful energies and entities, a gift that first emerged when he was just three years old. This rare talent led him to study with psychic masters across the globe—Afghanistan, France, Sweden, Israel, England, and Australia—each recognizing his unique gifts and helping him refine his craft.

In addition to his healing practice, Alex has practiced as a barrister, teacher, university lecturer, and small business owner, offering a well-rounded perspective on healing that combines spirituality with practical action. He is also an accomplished author, whose writings inspire and uplift readers by exploring the depths of human emotion and the power of self-healing.

Through his sessions, Alex has helped countless individuals overcome emotional turmoil and reclaim their lives. His work transcends cultural and geographical boundaries, offering profound healing to those in need. His mission is simple yet powerful: to guide people back to their authentic selves, helping them live with purpose, peace, and fulfillment.

With a career built on compassion, wisdom, and deep spiritual insight, Alex remains a beacon of hope for anyone seeking to overcome their struggles and wanting to step into a life of clarity and joy.

Other Titles by Alex Telman

Non Fiction
Think Like a Modern Guru
Mastering Hypnosis: Complete Step-by-Step Manual, Case Studies, and Sample Scripts
From Cursed to Cured: 100 True Stories of Healing from Curses
Connecting to the Afterlife: a how-to guide
Your Journey from Death to Rebirth
Empower Your Sundays: Unlocking Inner Strength for a Resilient Life
The Truth Behind the Creation Story: A Journey Through Reincarnation
Practical Mentalism in a Nutshell
Reprogram Your Mind in a Nutshell
Meditation in a Nutshell
Alex Telman in Quotes

Novels
A Happy Death
One Life, Half Lived
Down and Out in Byron Bay
God Speaks: A Journey Through Creation in His Own Words
Jesus Speaks: The Man Behind the Miracle in His Own Words

Poetry
Telman: The Complete Haiku 1974-2024
Echoes of September 11

CONGRATULATIONS! YOU'RE STILL A MESS

Homeless in New York
Burning Echoes of Time
From Dawn to Dusk: the life cycle in sonnets
Eternal Echoes: The Tapestry of Time and the Unseen
Snapshots of People I Have Never Met
Legends and Lessons: 36 Myths Unveiled
A Measure of Time: The Eternal Voyage of Self
Ashes of Verses: Poems Burned But Not Forgotten
Reflections on Solitude: A Poetic Journey Through The Lonely Mind
Your Friendship is a Museum
Whispers to Bella

Don't miss out!

Visit the website below and you can sign up to receive emails whenever Alex Telman publishes a new book. There's no charge and no obligation.

https://books2read.com/r/B-A-YBSCC-HOGMF

BOOKS 2 READ

Connecting independent readers to independent writers.